Theodore Dreiser

THE GIANT

Wayne F Burke

ISBN: 978-93-6354-271-6

First Edition: 2024
Rs. 200/-

Cyberwit.net
HIG 45 Kaushambi Kunj, Kalindipuram
Allahabad - 211011 (U.P.) India
http://www.cyberwit.net
Tel: +(91) 9415091004
E-mail: info@cyberwit.net

Printed at Repro India Limited.

INTRODUCTION

I first picked-up Theodore Dreiser's AN AMERICAN TRAGEDY, his masterpiece, via a five-finger discount from the back cupboard of room 101, where the high school English classes met. I stuffed the fat paperback volume into my duffle-bag after having wandered from the empty hallway into the empty classroom, while on my way out the school after basketball practice. I put the stolen book on the shelf of my bedroom bookcase, beside a dozen other books I had acquired, some of which I had read: THE EXORCIST, by William P. Blatty; THE HOUND OF THE BASKERVILLES by A. Conan Doyle; and A SEPARATE PEACE by John Knowles (for Sophomore English).

Steeped, as I then was, in Sophomorean ignorance, I wondered who would or could read such a hefty tome as the TRAGEDY. The size of it! Thick as three books. The length of it discouraged me from even opening. The book, consequently, sat like an ornament and collected dust for half-a-dozen years. Only after I had dropped out of college, for a 2nd time, and while bored nearly out my mind (living in my hometown again, in my grandmother's apartment) did I pick-up Dreiser's opus, which, serendipitously, had remained in my possession.

Reading the TRAGEDY not only killed time—which I dearly needed, at this point in my life, to slay; but like all great literature, took me out of myself by allowing me entrance to an alternative world.

From a certain unnamed American city, the story moved to Kansas City, Kansas; Chicago and New York. I tagged along with the hapless protagonist/hero of Dreiser's imagining, Clyde Griffths, a poor boy navigating through life more or less like a leaf blown by strong winds.

The hunger of Clyde to live and enjoy; his struggle to escape stultifying and confining conditions of his birth; his subsequent rise to minor prominence in his Uncle's factory in Lycurgus, N.Y.; the burden of his illicit love for the factory-girl, Roberta Alden—a flower grown from a mud heap of a farm; his duplicity after abandoning the tenets of his folk's religion, and listening to an efrit—genii, spirit— perching on his shoulder as he contemplated murder; the elegance and desirability, to Clyde, of beautiful Sondra Finchley, pampered siren of wealth & comfort; the awesome heart ache of love lost! The pitiable ache of the bleeding heart! The excitement of new love and fruit of what money can buy; the dastardly deed...Unspeakable...Unthinkable...

And yet—

I cried for Roberta during that first reading (first of a half-dozen) and also for Clyde, and like Etta Barnes in THE BULWARK, for life too; the vagaries of the human heart—which were Dreiser's subject: the heart strings, systole and diastole of the organ; beating for life—more life! For love too.

My most recent reading of the book completed nearly dry-eyed, and with less sympathy for Roberta than I had previously felt. Could not she have gone off by herself instead of demanding Clyde marry her? Could she not have made some sort of deal whereby she be recompensed through wealth Clyde were to accrue via marriage to the rich girl? Maybe so, I thought; but possibly not either: not as trapped as she was by her conventional upbringing and religious indoctrination. The weight of convention on her; her fear of the shame should she be exposed as pregnant and unmarried; the horror, to her, of that state! Less sympathy for Clyde as well, who, after all, perpetrated the crime—no matter how unwittingly completed. Accidentally or not, he responsible for her death; he the agent (though society at fault as well). But he trapped too—by his own desires; his pursuit of dreams his errant heart dictated—dreams inoculated in his poor deprived youth; dreams for place and pleasure, beauty and wealth, love and sensuality...The American dream of success before him but always, seemingly, just beyond reach of his fingertips...He was shuffled back and forth by social conventions, mores of a society he was too eager to gain entrance too. Oh but simultaneously with the dreams, the cravenness and duplicity of his scheming! His deplorable plotting of the demise of his sweetheart! The cold dialectical reasoning of his design! The evil thereof—

And yet—and yet—

Through sheer accumulative weight of thought, feeling, machination—and wealth of details—Dreiser moved Clyde ever closer to the reprehensible act. The thoughts, feelings, making the deed wholly believable—the verisimilitude the triumph of the TRAGEDY. Triumph of Dreiser's imagination and skill in so thoroughly revealing, through adumbration, mind and mood of a boy, limited in intellect, but savvy enough—evil or sick enough—influenced enough—to plot murder, and in his bungling way, carry it, or a facsimile of it, out.

Tsk! Tsk! Tsk!

The electric chair down the hall from the cellblock, awaiting those who strayed from the path of righteousness: Old Sparky. The lights of the cell block blinked on and off whenever the switch would be pulled.

Dreiser's characters—Clyde, Roberta, Carrie, Jennie, Cowperwood, Eugene, Hurstwood, Solon, Stewart, Etta, Aileen, et al., run the gamut of human emotion. Carrie Meeber, in her rocking chair, alonc and lonely despite wealth and celebrity; Hurstwood in his flop-house room, with the gas turned on; Jennie Gerhardt's melancholy reverie after a parade of dead loved ones...Poor and rich mixed in the melting pot of Dreiser's America. Land of the Pilgrim's pride perhaps, but humble land of contradiction as well—of inequality—bitterly divisive—founded on a current of xenophobia, anti-intellectualism, and racism (as illustrated in the greatest American novel, HUCKLEBERRY FINN). Land of liberty for some and enslavement for others; justice for some, injustice for others. Land of humankind's greatest hope and some of her darkest fears.

The TRAGEDY best known of Dreiser's novels, and the one made him most money—$50,000 in royalties alone from Horace Liveright, publisher. $135,000 more from various Hollywood studios. The book's popularity enhanced by the 1951 film "A Place in the Sun," a forgettable production, despite gathering six Academy Awards (Shelly Winters horribly miscast as Robert Alden).

Dreiser wrote six other novels, a host of short stories, poetry, plays, memoirs, philosophical tracts, and journalism. An out-pouring of Niagara Falls-like production. Superhuman productivity—leading me to title my study THE GIANT.

Herein could be found explication, exegesis, and synopses (short and long) of each novel, much of the nonfiction, and some of the short stories—with reference, as needed, to work in other genres. Between synopses the life of Dreiser in late 19th century America and to mid-point of the 20th century.

Contents

HOOSIERS

Herman Theodore Dreiser's father, John Paul Dreiser, born in Mayen, Germany, along the Moselle River, come to America in 1844 to avoid military conscription; he 23-years old. Theodore Dreiser's mother, Sarah Dreiser nee Schanab, born in 1833, and grown in Ohio, USA—born in Dayton (pg. 20, Lingeman, Richard, THEODORE DREISER, At the Gate of the City, vol. 1). Daughter of Mennonites (Dunkards). She and John Paul met in Fort Wayne, Indiana (pg. 20, Lingemen, vol. 1) where the Schanab's had relocated, from Ohio. The couple married against the wishes of Sarah's father. She, 16-years old, and he, John Paul, twenty-seven.

Theodore Dreiser was born August 27, 1871, in Terre Hault, Indiana, a "smoky town on the Wabash River," of 17,000 inhabitants (pg. 3, Swanberg, W.A., DREISER). The eleventh child in a family of thirteen (first 3-children died in infancy). A sickly baby, by Theodore's own account.

The family never stayed very long in any one place—five different addresses in Terre Hault—though making an auspicious debut in Sullivan, Indiana, where the elder Dreiser bought into a woolen mill. Prosperity the family experienced in Sullivan was short lived however, as the father lost the business through incompetence, chicanery, or both. Moving from Sullivan, the family experienced a fall from grace and "expulsion from Eden of middle-class respectability" wrote Dreiser biographer Jerome Loving (pg. 26, THE LAST TITAN, A Life of Theodore Dreiser).

The family begun migrating around the state, living more or less on the "edge of town(s)" (pg. 8, James T. Farrell, introduction, THEODORE DREISER, His World and His Novels). The father seemingly more concerned, as parent, with the state of the children's souls in the hereafter than in their destinies in the here-and-now. He a markedly unsuccessful businessman, and ineffectual father—according to his son, Theo, who pitied the man as an incompetent and "mentally weak" human being (pg. 14, Lehan, Richard, THEODORE DREISER, His World and His Novels). The father's mill burnt down; he had also suffered a blow to the head by a fallen beam, badly injuring him.

Theodore, called "Dorsh," "Thee," and "Teddy" by the family, attended Parochial School on insistence of his father. Theo spent formative years in Sullivan, Indiana, living with his mother and younger siblings—after the mom split from the dad, for financial reasons (the dad remaining in Terre Hault with other of the children).

Paul Dreiser Junior, eldest of the brood, left home in his teens to become a minstrel-singer, comedian, and song writer. His songs, collected in "Paul Dresser's Song Book" (he Anglicized his last name) made him well-known. A gregarious fat man, standing 6-feet 1-inch tall and weighing 300-pounds in his heyday as a Broadway character and player. He had a big heart and out-sized personality (and an aversion to physical labor). "On the Banks of the Wabash, Far Away" become one of his biggest hit songs—its chorus, if not some lyrics, written by Theo.

Sent to Seminary by his father, Paul dropped-out and become truant, arrested for burglary, and other crimes, before escaping town with a traveling minstrel troupe. His returning, a few years later, a fortuitous event for the family who had descended into poverty. Paul shared his money freely; he also moved part of the family (mother's part) into a house he acquired in Evansville, Indiana—with help of his girlfriend, Sally Walker (a madam). The family remaining in Evansville nearly two years—until evicted by Sally after she and Paul split-up (pg. 4, Swanberg).

Dreiser never had to look much further than his family for material to use in his fiction-writing. The 2nd oldest Dreiser son, Rome, become an alcoholic drifter; sisters Emma, Mame, Theresa, and Sylvia, stayed busy "playing off romantic tangents" (pg. 59, Lingemen, vol. 1). Their multiplicity of affairs and complications resulting brought disrepute to the family from so-called respectable others. Mame's trouble in a liaison with a married man would later be used by Dreiser as plot-line of his first novel SISTER CARRIE.

Sarah and kids, and both Paul's, father and son, made a "go" of it in Chicago, Illinois, but with the city proving too expensive for their means, the mother, with three of her youngest children, returned to Warsaw, Indiana. The year: 1884. Theo 13-years old. Both Paul's sent support money. Theo, Ed, and Claire (Tillie) the youngest of the brood enrolled in Public School—against their father's wishes. The father's insistence on the children's attendance of Parochial School, plus his tithing to the Catholic Church, contributing to the family's frequent poverty-stricken condition. A condition Theo blamed his father for and cause of an ever-widening breech between father and son.

At sixteen Theo quit school. And becoming sick of the provincialism of Warsaw and his exclusion by the "better," wealthier, children of the town, decamping for Chicago. (An exclusion that turned him to solitary pursuits, reading, writing, and long walks communing with nature.) As he left, his mother handed him 3-dollars and a lunch (pg 70, Lingeman, vol.1)

CITY OF TOO BIG SHOULDERS

Dreiser hoped, dreamed, to make-it on his own in the big city. After securing a rooming house room he searched for work, taking the only job offered: dishwasher. Unable to support himself however, on a pearl-diver's salary, he turned to family members, who in turn, summoned the mom, Sarah, to the city.

Settled into a 35-dollar a month flat, Theo, Mame, Al, Theresa, Ed, and Tillie attempted to support each other and mom. The peripatetic Rome Dreiser also showed, on his way elsewhere ("dead by forty in a Chicago dive," wrote F.O Matthiessen pg. 12, THEODORE DREISER. "Dead about 1905," Dreiser claimed in A HOOSIER HOLIDAY. Neither were right. Rome lived to old age and was installed in Dreiser's home at the end).

What a fortuitous day for Theo when his favorite Warsaw Public School teacher, Miss Fielding, approached him in Chicago with an offer he could not refuse: a year at Indiana State University! Along with a stipend supplied by her (pg. 69, Lingeman, vol. 1). Miss Fielding, working as a principle in a Chicago school, knew the President of the University and was able to gain Dreiser admission, without his holding a high school diploma, entering as a "special" student.

Dreiser arrived in Bloomington carrying a single suitcase and wearing his brother's hand-me-down suit. Theo could not however, become very excited by learning or the learned of the college. He proved but a fair student scholastically and did minimal amount of course-work. He had gone in for exploring local caves and for rapturous gazing at co-eds—but too bashful to approach any.

Meanwhile, back in Chicago, the mother died, aged fifty-seven. Her death bringing on a collapse of the family: without a center the circumference broke.

Theo did not return to school for a second year (though offered one by Miss Fielding—pg. 20, Matthiesson). He returned to Chicago and begun tramping the oily streets, unemployed and broke.

After enough tramping, he secured a job as driver for a large laundry concern—a job Clyde Griffths of the TRAGEDY held, after going on the lam from K.C. After the laundry gig come a job as bill-collector of money owed by people suckered into pay-on-installment plan buying. In between jobs and working Theo wrote impressionistic prose pieces he submitted to newspapers, but with no luck publishing (pg. 87, Lingeman, vol.1).

Having saved $65, Theo and younger brother Ed and their sister Tillie (each of whom walked a slightly straighter path than the others) moved away from the father and other siblings. Theo had set his sights on becoming a newspaper reporter and to this end begun hanging around the offices of the Chicago Globe, eventually being hired by the Globe as part-timer and sent to cover the Democratic national Convention, then in town. Due to solid work on the convention, the paper hired him full-time.

Dreiser considered his sexual life, at this time, unsatisfactory. He had been bothered, or distressed, by premature ejaculation (pg. 99, Lingeman, vol. 1). His anxiety over impregnating a woman, plus his fear of sexually transmitted disease served him, one biographer wrote, “as (a) psychic coitus-interruptus” (pg. 100, Lingeman, vol. 1).

A editor friendly to him on the Chicago Globe recommended Theo go to work for the Saint Louis Democrat—to make better money and work for a superior newspaper.

Once in Saint Louis, Theo’s sexual anxiety abated through experiences with two accommodating landladies he rented from. Dreiser’s big break as reporter come when a train crashed into some tanker cars full of oil. He had rushed on-scene and wrote, on his own initiative, a first-person account of the horror-inducing scene. His salary, as consequence, increased, as did respect from other writers and editors.

Wishing to get away from reporting on death, poverty, crime, and charred remains, Theo applied for a part-time post as the newspaper's theater critic. The job brought him to be asked to chaperone a bevy of mid-western school teachers—beauties selected on a popularity basis—to the World's Fair of 1893, held in Chicago.

Talk of putting the fox in charge of the hen house! Among the prize-winners a young woman from Danville, Missouri, Sara White, nicknamed 'Jug' (why not "Jugs"?) whom Dreiser took an inordinate interest in. A young woman of "innocence and maidenly reserve" (pg. 118, Lingeman, vol. 1). She twenty-four years old—to Theo's twenty-one.

Returning to Saint Louis, Dreiser begun writing Sara, or Sallie, via snail-mail. An epistolary assault conjuring her love, while his lust simmered. When they next met, at a neutral venue, she played the piano for him—but nothing else (refusing to sit on his lap). She had, at this meeting, agreed to an informal engagement.

Theo's brother Paul, of the sentimental song, urged Theo to come east to NYC and see the sights. Paul also expressed displeasure with the maid from Missouri, warning Theo that a conventionally-minded church-going gal like Jug would trap him a conventional churchly marriage.

Theo meanwhile, growing restless in Saint Louis longed to see the greater world: He resigned his position and headed east to bigger things, he hoped, than even the World's Fair.

GO EAST YOUNG MAN

Theo landed in Grand Rapids, Michigan, where a hoped-for job as newspaper co-owner, fell through. He continued giving vent to his emotions in long, 50 and 60-page letters, to Jug in Missouri—a "creative drive," Richard Lingeman remarked, "powered by erotic energy" (pg. 126, Lingeman, vol. 1).

Next stop Toledo, Ohio, and visit to the Toledo Blade newspaper office where Dreiser engaged with an editor, Arthur Henry, formerly a Chicago newspaper man. Henry, like Dreiser, had literary ambitions; he steered some freelance work Dreiser's way but had no full-time job to offer. Henry would later play an important role in Dreiser's literary career. In A HOOSIER HOLIDAY Dreiser wrote of his relationship to Henry as an "enduring and yet stormy and disillusioning friendship" (pg. 254, AHH). The pair's dreams, Dreiser also wrote, "practically identical" yet approached from different angles.

On to Cleveland, Ohio. Where Dreiser would place his Gerhardt family, of his novel JENNIE GERHARDT. But little work for Theo there so he shuffled off to Buffalo, N.Y. (with a side trip to Niagara Falls, which made him "nauseous" (pg. 128, Lingeman, vol. 1)). From Buffalo on to Pittsburgh, Pennsylvania, and a job with the Pittsburgh Dispatch newspaper.

After work hours or during slow periods in Pittsburgh Dreiser read at one of Carnegie's libraries. His reading of Balzac's work inspired him to conceive of also writing a Comedie Humaine, American version. The work of Balzac and philosophy of Herbert Spenser made vivid impressions on Dreiser's intellectual development, forming the basis and inspiration of his thought processes.

In the summer Dreiser migrated back to Missouri to visit Jug, and then, on invitation, to NYC to visit his brother Paul.

In the city Theo stayed with disgraced sister, Emma, and her husband, who had been caught stealing from an employer and absconding (like Hurstwood in SISTER CARRIE). Both were being subsidized by Paul, rolling in dough through sales of his music (pg. 138, Lingeman, vol. 1).

Paul gave Theo a tour of the million-eyed robotic city that never slept; he took Theo to a French bordello, "La Fellatio." Theo left for return to Pittsburgh determined to save money for a return to NYC.

At this time, Theo, at six-foot-one inches tall, weighing 140-pounds (pg. 142, Lingeman, vol. 1) was described as "gangling" and "spindly" (pg. 106, Swanberg). After socking away $240 he returned to NYC, great megalopolis, and went back to living with Emma and her husband, Hopkins, a disgraced Tammany hall politician-crook who had once turned his and Emma's flat into a house of assignation. Hopkins was down-and-out at this time period, in the same spiral that would take Dreiser's George Hurstwood down the drain in SISTER CARRIE.

Theo helped Emma and her children move out of Hopkin's shadow. Meanwhile, unable to get along well working at space rate for the WORLD Newspaper, Theo quit, vowing to never again do newspaper work.

A bad time to quit—the depression of 1893 was on and untold thousands out on the streets dependent upon charity, of which there was little. Dreiser bided time among the down-and-out in the park, waiting for his brother, Paul, to return from being on tour. Theo's period in the park gave him much material for later journalistic efforts and usage in his novels.

Paul introduced Theo to Howley & Haviland (pg. 164, Lingeman, vol. 1), the company promoting and selling Paul's songs—saccharine and nostalgic ballads like "The Pardon Came Too Late," "Just Tell them that You Saw Me," and "My Gal Sal." Making use of well-worn tropes of motherhood, and the good ole days, and love lost or found…The Company published an in-house organ called "Ev'ry Month." Paul's influence got Theo hired as editor of the publication, a job he kept two years, publishing much of his own writing (wrote most of first two issues) as well as work of other worthies, including Stephen Crane and Bret Hardt. Subscription and distribution increased dramatically under Theo but with small profit to the Company.

According to Richard Lingeman, Theo wrote the first verse of Paul's hit song "On the Banks of the Wabash," and perhaps the chorus (Paul never crediting his brother's assistance). "On the Banks of the Wabash" become the Indiana State Song in 1913.

Following Ev'ry Month, Dreiser turned to magazine-writing. Working beside his writing-buddy Arthur Henry, the two crashed the magazine market, becoming successful freelance contributors making as much as $5000 yearly ($50,000 in today's money). Success Magazine published and paid Dreiser for thirty articles, at $100 a pop.

ON THE BANKS OF THE MAUMEE RIVER

Theo and Jug's 4-year long courtship ended in December of 1898 when Jug, aged twenty-nine, agreed to elope. The couple married in Washington DC, in a Methodist minister's office (pg. 208, Lingeman, vol. 1). The unsatisfied Dreiser—with his constantly yearning heart—now had a wife as well as new mother (matronly Jug) fulfilling his maternal yearning. The couple set-up house in an apartment at 6 West 102nd Street (pg. 210, Lingeman, vol. 1). Sara cooked, cleaned, and put out the Lord of the Manor's underwear, socks, and slippers—also slept with him—though during the long courtship Theo's ardor for her had cooled. Jug also took dictation whenever Theo's hand faltered or mind wandered from tasks at hand. She also played, Arthur Henry-like, a collaborative role in production of Dreiser's first two novels, CARRIE and JENNIE. The extent of her collaboration unclear.

City friends, colleagues of Theo's, did not know what to make of the new wife—provincial in outlook, she allowed no alcohol served at parties in their apartment. The associates, chums, were however glad to eat, by the pound, Jug's famous biscuits.

In the summer Dreiser and wife took residence with Arthur Henry and his wife Maude (also a writer) on the bank of the Maumee River in the village of Maumee, Ohio. The two women busied themselves cooking and cleaning while the menfolk took to composition.

With Henry's encouragement Dreiser got off a poetry kick he had been on (unsuccessfully submitting to publishers) in order to write prose.

One of Theo's first efforts—and his first published short story—titled "McEwen of the Shining Slave Masters"—a tale in which a man turned into an ant (or did he? Could be but vivid dream—like Kafka's

Gregor Samsa dreamt). The man, now ant, become involved in a raging ant war between tribes. Interestingly, he along with fellow ants of his acquaintance, fight without fear of being killed or injured; without ANY emotion—pure unemotional instinct governing their actions. None fret with anxiety, or brood on morality or mortality, obedient only to an inbred certainty: how unlike humankind! A different state of being—wholly convincing, though obviously a "fantasy."

Another of Dreiser's stories—and his second published story, "Nigger Jeff," become a Dreiser classic. "His finest short story of the pre-SISTER CARRIE period," wrote Jerome Loving (pg. 36, THE LAST TITAN). Not a racist story—despite the unfortunate title, but tale of great humanity—at least on the part of the narrator-reporter. (In early years Dreiser did refer to blacks as "darkies." Also, in a 1916 diary entry he wrote—while on a trip from NYC to Savannah, Georgia—"segregation of blacks an odd but necessary system" (pg. 200, Swanberg)).

Dreiser wrote five Maumee stories over the summer before returning to NYC. Henry, working on his own fiction, returned to the city with Theo and Jug, leaving Maude alone to hold down the fort in Ohio.

Thee and bud set-up shop in the Dreiser's new apartment and begun cranking-out articles for the popular press, as well as doing their own work, hoping to make enough money from the hack-work to enable them to work exclusively at the business of literature, specifically fiction-writing.

Henry and Theo needed each other: both had dreams too big for only one man. Dreiser fed off Henry's dreams, and vice-versa. Henry provided valuable editing experience and assistance pruning the fecund Dreiser's ungovernable prose. Henry shepherd SISTER CARRIE ("masterpiece of reportorial realism"—pg. 145, Loving) to the publishing firm of Doubleday and Page.

Doubleday's reader Frank Norris, author of the ground-breaking work of realistic-fiction McTEAGUE (1899), very much liked Dreiser's book, and advised his employer to publish. Dreiser had admired McTEAGUE; wrote that the novel "the first real American book I ever read" (pg. 154, Loving).

Norris, along with Stephen Crane, and to some extent, Hamlin Garland, had made tremendous inroads into the Genteel Tradition of letters predominating 19th century American literature. The above mentioned trio's interjection of realism into the flow shocked the grandma's of literary expression—self-proclaimed guardians of woman's virtue and apologists for a class system of rank exploitation of the masses. Reactionaries, who had led the nation into an elitist culture.

Garland was best known to literary history for his short story collection MAIN-TRAVELED ROADS (1891). A work that brought in the vernacular speech of mid-western farm and working folk to American literature. The "Dean" of American literature, at the time, William Dean Howells, an exponent of "polite realism," and the period's most influential critic, wrote of Garland's stories containing a "tragic sublimity." Howell's also wrote of the amorality of the endings of some Garland stories. Like the Naturalists to follow, Garland was not overly concerned with conventional morality (not in 1891 he wasn't—but later aligned himself with Philistines in opposition to Naturalism). Garland's characters gave voice to a hitherto ignored or else patronized segment of the U.S. populace, putting into the speech of his characters the inflections and ungrammatical nuances of their language—thus gave his folk a dignity previously rendered sentimentally or stereotypically.

Stephen Crane's MAGGIE: A Girl of the Streets, turned into a prophetic work in predicting the future of American literature. The work a sort of bridge connecting the realism of W.D. Howells and others to that of the Naturalists following (Dreiser, Dos Passos). Crane's prose style of carefully fashioned similes and metaphors and frequent personification of inanimate life, was full of a rough-hewn poetry. The prose had an affinity to Impressionistic painting in Crane's frequent use of color to signify and heighten expressiveness of his language. Crane's tale more deterministic than Dreiser's in that the characters of MAGGIE do not aspire to escape their environment—do not even consider escape possible. They are stuck, without hope, without possibility of redemption, and without the high aspirations of Dreiser's characters. Maggie of MAGGIE, Richard Lehan pointed out (pg. 252) "is as much a victim of her moral turpitude as she is of her environment."

Crane more the conscious artist than his successors. His work could be said to mark the end of Realism as much as marking beginnings of American Naturalism.

W. D. Howells, a remote-Realist (most realistic novel A HAZARD OF NEW FORTUNES) had been instrumental in having Crane's work put before the public. Crane along with Norris (until he, like Garland, did a flip-flop) led the fight against establishmentarian elders among the crowd of fossilized relics governing the byways of public discourse in 19th and early 20th centuries.

With his first novel Dreiser wandered into the no-man's land of the on-going battle between so-called Realists and traditionalists. Frank Doubleday, half owner of the firm, was quondam Realist; had, after all, published McTEAGUE (Doubleday and McClure). But Frank was not, apparently, able to handle Dreiser's brand of realism. After agreeing to publish Dreiser's novel, Doubleday reversed himself (under influence of his wife Dreiser later claimed—a story Jerome Loving and others called false). Dreiser however, insisted Doubleday stick to the contract agreed upon, and publish. The firm, under legal duress, printed copies but made little effort to distribute or publicize the work, thereby ensuring the book's anemic sales figures (though Frank Norris sent out, on his own initiative, 100-plus review copies).

W. D. Howells did not, reportedly, like Dreiser's novel. "(Howells) won't see American life as it is," Dreiser wrote: "He doesn't want to see it" (pg. 57, Matthiessen).

CARRIE went almost un-reviewed in the U. S. but after a truncated version was published in England, laudatory reviews poured in from English critics (a similar course as happened to Melville's MOBY DICK).

Finished in 1900 and published in 1900 SISTER CARRIE sold 500 copies in the U. S. and 1500 of the condensed English version, published by Heineman.

SISTER CARRIE

Carrie Meeber, that is. Eighteen years old. From Columbia Point, Wisconsin, which she left for Chicago, Illinois, a few hours distant by train.

Entrained, she made acquaintance of a traveling salesman, a Drummer; one Charles Drouet. Their meeting brief; he promising to call on her at her sister's place, where Carrie would stay in the city.

The sister, Minnie, older than Carrie, lived a life circumscribed by conditions of financial and spiritual poverty, with an uncommunicative working-stiff husband, Sven, and their infant child.

Carrie left the flat to search for employment. She barely managing addressing strangers in her job-search. Her courage nearly giving way. She was helped however by her prettiness—helped with males anyway. One of them hired her to work as a machine operator in a shoe manufacturing operation. Carrie found the job monotonous, repetitive—the hours long, pay minimal.

Outside of work, life at the sister's was dull for Carrie. The Hanson's unimaginative, and tired—working people stuck in unvarying routine (Sven cleaned refrigerator cars).

Following a spell of illness, Carrie lost her job. Out searching for another she met Drouet, he of the train ride (the novel full of chance meetings—in Dreiser's world of chance). A sharper, or masher type—"a merry unthinking, moth of the flame," Dreiser wrote. He took Carrie to lunch. She, broke and hungry. He won her allegiance with presentation of "two soft, green, handsome ten dollar bills."

The drummer offered Carrie a way out her unendurable life with the Hansons. She allowed him to guide her to a furnished room and to pay for odds and ends.

Winter was coming.

Carrie become a kept-woman, sharing Drouet's 3-room flat. She wanted the legitimacy of marriage but Drouet put her off with vague promises.

Something of a man-about-town, Drouet frequented certain popular semi-exclusive eating and drinking establishments of the city—where he tried to ingratiate himself with established personages. At one such, he had become friendly with the saloon manager, one George Hurstwood. Wishing to deepen his connection, by impressing the manager, Drouet introduced the man to Carrie. The well-to-do manager, something of a bon vivant, had a certain savoir faire the Drummer lacked—which was obvious to Carrie, impressed by Hurstwood's manner. To her, Drouet paled in comparison with socially-adept and prosperous-appearing George.

Slowly, in guise of friendship and geniality, Hurstwood made the Drummer his dupe.

Now and again a voice of omniscience, prophetic-sounding, solemn and sepulchral—also occasionally cruelly ironic (pg. 79, Lehan), intruded into the narrative. These asides, made off-stage, alert the reader to a controlling hand moving the vehicle—the story. A teller behind the tale. Present as an unknown god.

Hurstwood wormed his way into the apple of Carrie's heart. Doing so with little to no reflection on his wife and two children at home. A wife he considered "cold, self-centered," and "dull"—certainly no match for Carrie in the beauty or personality departments. This obliviousness of Hurstwood would later cost him dearly.

The little shop-girl meanwhile, under tutelage of a friendly neighbor, Mrs. Hale, a fashionable and au courant young mother, was learning style and making herself more presentable to the world at large. She was also developing a hitherto unmentioned dreamy wistfulness, indulging in perverse pleasure bouts of brooding.

Inflamed by the girl's youthful freshness—her enticing lack of rapacity and guile—Hurstwood declared his love for her and she responded favorably.

The cuckolded Drouet, happening to belong to the Elks Club which happened to be in need of an actress to appear in the club's theatrical, volunteered Carrie. Though dubious as to her acting abilities, she took to the occasion like a duck to water, becoming star of the amateur production. (She an "emotional genius" Dreiser wrote.)

Hurstwood, an Elk as well, was in attendance at the play.

Because of a certain enthusiasm in Hurstwood's manner, Drouet begun to suspect the saloon-manager's attentions to Carrie as not disinterested ones.

Hurstwood convinced Carrie to go away with him—leaving Drouet. He also promised her marriage.

However: Mrs. Hurstwood—who, by the way, had her husband's holdings in her name—had also caught the fragrant and flagrant scent of her husband's illicit dalliance. She confronted George, and fire-works ensued—George wilting under the barrage of his wife's scorn. Understanding he had acted precipitately—had he ever! But unable to check his enthusiasm, George retreated to mull-over options after his wife mentioned divorce.

It seemed odd, at this point in the narrative—Carrie on verge of leaving Drouet for Hurstwood—that she unaware Hurstwood was married. Only learning the fact when Drouet confronted her with his suspicions about the saloon-manager's intentions toward her.

After the confrontation, Drouet left the flat in a funk—with Carrie unsure if he would be returning.

Alone again: what should she do? She vowed never to have anything else to do with Hurstwood. After the duplicity. A married man!

Meanwhile, Hurstwood heard from the lawyer his wife had engaged and begun divorce proceedings. He knew that in the procedure he would lose everything—his net-worth of $40,000.

While closing up the establishment one night, as was Hurstwood's wont, he discovered the safe left open. An odd oversight by someone. For some reason, perhaps because a little fogged by over-indulging in alcohol, instead of closing and locking the safe, he removed and counted the $10,000 therein. Suddenly, as he counted, a voice whispered in his ear—an efrit perhaps—the voice that would speak to Clyde Griffths as he pondered murder—a spirit, sprite, demon perhaps, urging Hurstwood into action inimical to his well-being. He pocketed the cash. A mad act!

Knowing the theft would be discovered in the morning, he hatched an equally mad plan.

Taking a cab to Carrie's flat, he told her Drouet had had an accident and was in the hospital. After rushing Carrie into the cab, he instructed the driver to go to the train station. At the station he bought two tickets, and still using the ruse of Drouet's accident, ushered Carrie aboard. As the train sped toward Detroit and, putatively, Drouet, Carrie protested. Hurstwood was able to mollify her, and in Detroit the two entrained for Montreal.

In Montreal Hurstwood told Carrie she was now his wife.

In a Montreal hotel Hurstwood was confronted by a private-dick. Hurstwood agreed to return most of the stolen money if his ex-employer did not prosecute. He and Carrie then moving on to N.Y.C. where Hurstwood spent the better part of his remaining cash buying into a saloon-business.

He and Carrie begun leading a modest existence.

Carrie become friendly with her neighbor, Mrs. Vance (another significant neighbor!) whose friendship provided Carrie an inside-look at high-living—as guest of the well-to-do Vance's, to fancy restaurants and theaters.

Through the Vances' Carrie met one Rob Ames, an intellectual and something of an "artist"—though called himself "inventor." Ames the first artist/intellectual type Carrie met. He gave her, Dreiser wrote, an "ideal" to henceforth use in contrasting and comparing manhood.

3-years passed. The saloon that 43-year old Hurstwood become part owner of was sold out from under him. The sale and subsequent trial of earning a living begun a downward slide for George, his money trickling away. Searching for a new position, but finding nothing commensurate to his talents (or pocketbook), he become discouraged. His attitude obviously was all wrong: not presenting himself as supplicant, in his job search, but with the grand air once assumed as manager of Fizgerald & Moys's Saloon, back in Chicago. A striking lack of humility in a job-seeker. He had never previously needed any—humility. Never had been broke previously either; had never known poverty.

After his loss of bravado, Hurstwood stopped searching; becoming morose, defeated; spending days hanging around the flat (a smaller place than that previously lived in—in a less expensive district).

In a desperate act, Hurstwood took up playing poker, card-playing. But playing poor-man's poker—close to the vest, wary of raising, chary of bluffing, put him at a distinct disadvantage and, unsurprisingly, he lost money he could not afford to lose. His precious, and dwindling bankroll thinning out.

Carrie meanwhile, becoming irritated by Hurstwood hanging about, plus making use of her money to pay rent and the grocery bill, went out seeking employment, landing a job as chorus-girl, at a salary of $12 weekly.

Feeling the humiliation of being supported by a woman, Hurstwood stirred himself once more to action, becoming driver of a trolley car during a strike of trolley-car drivers. A scab.

Assaulted during his shift, by striking workers, and deciding for discretion over valor, he quit.

Carrie, viewing Hurstwood's quitting unsympathetically, and as further evidence of he being obstinate, and perhaps lazy, decided to move out. Handing Hurstwood 20-dollars before moving, she went to live with a chorus-line girlfriend.

Of necessity, Hurstwood soon departed the flat for less expensive digs—until even a single room proving too expensive, and he went out into the streets and begun begging for money.

Carrie's salary soon rose to $150 weekly—she making a success of herself as actress in a Broadway comedy.

Bob Ames, the Vances's cousin, returning to the city, met Carrie again; he urging her to turn from comedy to dramatic acting to realize the full potential of her emotional genius.

Carrie mulled-over the suggestion.

Meanwhile, Hurstwood, sliding ever lower, finally gave up, turned the gas on in his flophouse room, and died.

Oblivious to Hurstwood's demise, and risen ever higher, Carrie sat, at story's end, in her rocking chair rocking and dreaming—of "such happiness" Dreiser wrote, as she "will never find."

Such the dreaming curse of the true Romantic! Alone in an un-Romantic world.

"The first Great American novel of the 20th century," wrote Jerome Loving (pg. 130, THE LAST TITAN). "First truly major step in literary democracy since Whitman and Twain."

DREISER REDUX

The sullied post-publication history of SISTER CARRIE sent Dreiser into a tailspin. He simply could not accept the novel's premature and, to him, inexplicable demise. He begun brooding over his and his book's seeming unsuccessful fate, and fell into inactivity.

Dreiser's buddy Henry invited Theo and Jug to live on an island off the coast of Connecticut; the island owned by Henry's new wife, Anna. The Thoreauvian experiment of being on Henry's "Dumpling Island" did not suit Dreiser. His brooding turned gloomy in "chill gray days" (pg. 314, Lingeman, vol. 1). Feeling as if his ambitions destroyed by the publishing debacle, Theo sunk dangerously toward apathy. He argued with Henry's Anna, as did Jug. She and Theo had liked Maude, first Henry wife, and perhaps subconsciously (and consciously) resented Anna for replacing her.

Dreiser and Jug returned to NYC. Theo's dreams undergone revision: instead of fame, money, and artistic glory he begun seeking "answers to social questions in the un-doctrinal sphere of social Christianity" (pg. 320, Lingeman, vol. 1). He also managed to interest a publisher, J. F. Taylor, in a new novel, JENNIE GERHARDT, receiving a $100 monthly stipend to bring the novel to completion. The firm also expressing interest in a revival of SISTER CARRIE. However, the publisher begun urging Dreiser to place a moralistic message within the text—an urge making Dreiser wonder if the Doubleday fiasco were to be played-out again.

He stopped work on JENNIE.

After a stay with Jug's family in Missouri, she and Theo toured the southern U. S., stopping in Red Sulphur Springs, West Virginia—because Dreiser had heard the water "good for insomnia" (pg. 331, Lingeman, vol.1), which had begun bothering him, along with restlessness and increasing moodiness.

After either separating from Jug, or she from him, Theo went on a 300-mile solo hiking trip.

Concentration had become progressively harder for Theo. He making a few dollars writing some journalism but penury approaching. Jug rejoined him but could do little to alleviate his increasing gloominess. He consulted a doctor and was diagnosed as suffering from "nervous exhaustion"—or, "neurasthenia" (pg. 343, Lingeman, vol. 1). A more accurate diagnosis Dreiser biographer Richard Lingeman suggested as "depression." Probably inherited, Lingeman also suggested, from his, Theo's, father (pg. 344, Lingeman, vol. 1). (Lingeman also considers possibilities Dreiser suffered from manic-depression—bi-polarity.)

DOWN AND OUT IN NEW YORK

Dreiser arrived in NYC alone, and with $32 in pocket (pg. 359, Lingeman, vol. 1). Living in a cheap room in a Hurstwood-like flophouse in Brooklyn, Dreiser drifted while taking, perhaps, Lingeman suggested, a "neurotic security in his 'fatalism'" (pg. 363, Lingeman, vol. 1). In his reduced state, things becoming queer—ordinary occurrences seeming invested with cosmic significance—a mix of dream and reality brought on by sleeplessness and malnutrition. Funny visions begun in a world out of whack…He showed-up on his sister Mame's doorstep for a feed.

Soon afterward, while Theo walked along Broadway in NYC he was spotted by his brother Paul. Neither had seen the other since a falling out a year or so previous. Paul thrust a bankroll at his brother, and extracted promise of a visit from his brother. Theo returning afterward to the Mills Hotel, "waystation for the indigent" (pg. 172, Loving) with $75 in pocket (pg. 105, Swanberg).

Shocked by his brother's scruffy appearance, Paul paid to send Theo to Muldoon's sanitarium, a health spa run like a boot camp for the "rich and intemperate" (pg. 174, Loving) by ex-military man Muldoon (aka "Bulldoon") acting as drill-sergeant, General, and coach, as he whipped out-of-shape neurasthenic men into presentable condition. (See "Culhane, The Solid Man," TWELVE MEN, Theodore Dreiser). The institute's regimen of daily exercise and discipline Dreiser credited with taking his mind off himself and his morbidly introspective tendency, thus starting him back on the road to health.

Brother Paul too a motivating force for Theo at this time, in both encouragement and money.

After some time at Muldoon's Theo went to work on a mason's crew—used by the foreman, whom Theo called Rourke in his published essay "The Mighty Rourke" (see TWELVE MEN), primarily for clerical duty.

Upon Jug's return east from Missouri, she and Theo took an apartment in the Bronx. With Paul's assist Theo begun writing for the New York Daily News. After being laid-off from the News he spent time writing AN AMATEUR LABORER (unpublished) but leaving the work in fragmentary state. (Richard Lingeman wrote that parts of the work equal to Melville's PIERRE).

Dreiser's descent into nihilism endangered his health and sanity, but changed values he previously held sacrosanct. Fame and wealth still desirable to him but no longer the things of real value in life: relationships, affection, friendships, and tenderness most valuable, most real—plus love; and awe too—that had always been a part of his character.

THE SILENT DECADE

As years passed, SISTER CARRIE more or less sat underground hissing like unexploded ordinance. A friend and admirer of Dreiser, Charles MacLean, coughed-up $500 to buy the book plates of CARRIE from J. F. Taylor Co. (whom Dreiser owed $750 for previous stipend payments). MacLean and Dreiser planned to start a publishing house with CARRIE, but plans fell through. Dreiser, as editor of Smith's Magazine, was on his way to financial solvency, the flophouse permanently left behind.

Paul Dresser meanwhile, had lost his fortune in the song and music business and though making a come-back with his last big hit, "My Gal Sal," fell into disrepute and ended-up living with his sister Emma. Grossly overweight, suffering from a host of ailments—including syphilis—and depressed over his fall from grace, Paul died, aged forty-six—possibly from the mercury treatment he received in the 1880's (pg. 102, Loving). Dying penniless, after squandering, on himself and others, untold thousands.

As things got hot for Theo at Smith's Magazine, he decamped for Broadway Magazine, a rag-zine along the lines of latter day Police Gazette, and with an anemic circulation.

Dreiser, managing to transform the magazine, brought circulation up from 12,000 to 100,000. The zine becoming a magazine celebrating NYC, precursor to Vanity Fair and The New Yorker. Theo and Jug slid into bourgeois comfort in an apartment on Morningside Heights (pg. 408, Lingeman, vol. 1).

Ensconced in an ornate 12th floor office of the Butterick Building—while 2,000 underpaid workers labored—mostly on patterns—on lower floors (pg. 139, Swanberg)—Dreiser sat behind and on his editor's throne, folding and unfolding a handkerchief—as was his wont (a behavior thought to be helpful to him in dealing with anxiety), and rendering executive decisions to thirty-two underlings (pg. 120, Swanberg) whenever called upon—to the tune of $8,000 yearly.

SISTER CARRIE WAKES

Through a literary agent Dreiser's cashiered novel went into the hands of B. W. Dodge & Co. The caveat to their republication of CARRIE being Dreiser's purchase of fifty shares of stock in the company—or $5,000. The book reissued, by Dodge, in 1907. Copies sold eventually reaching 8,500 (pg. 416, Lingeman, vol. 1). A year later a paperback edition put out by Crosset & Dunlap sold 5,000 additional copies (pg. 187, Loving).

Dreiser's personal life in these early century years underwent revision. Grown tired of his wife, viewing her as impediment to his lifestyle, conventionally-minded Juggie though cultured and charming, objected to various types tolerant and open-minded Theo entertained. Particularly, persons of color (pg. 192, Loving). Also objected to Theo's sexual "varietism." Dreiser felt the wife crimping him, holding him back. (There had been no children because Dreiser practiced coitus interruptus—or was he sterile?—pg. 193, Loving).

In the fall of 1909 Dreiser got hot pants for the 17-year old daughter of a Butterick assistant, Annie Cudlipp. Dreiser's lecherous pursuit of the girl (Thelma) alarmed the mother who whisked the girl out of state. Intercepting Dreiser's love letters to her daughter, the mother demanded he ceased pursuit. After he refused—and was on the verge of leaving his wife for Thelma, the mother made a public outcry and consequently Dreiser lost his position with the Butterick Company. Fired.

In 1910 Theo and Jug separated. Theo thereby lost not only a sexual partner—though the relationship had cooled considerably—but a matronly figure, as well as part-time secretary, who organized his life.

Cut free from editorship responsibilities, Dreiser wrote his new friend H. L. Mencken—who had been a contributor to The Delineator (another magazine Dreiser edited) that he would finish his long-abandoned second novel—which he did, finish, in February of 1911. Mencken read a draft of JENNIE GERHARDT and wrote Dreiser "it seems to me to be sound…I get a powerful effect of reality, stark and unashamed" (pg. 38, Lingeman, Richard, THEODORE DREISER, An American Journey, 1908-1945, vol. 2).

JENNIE GERHARDT

Introduced was a facsimile of the Dreiser family, only called 'Gerhardts.' An ineffectual father—a glassblower temporarily out of work; a rock-solid mother; and a brood of children, six in all, including Rome Dreiser-like Sabastian ("Bass"), 18-year old Jennie, and descending age-wise, George, Martha, William, and Veronica the 8-year old 'baby' of the family.

Jennie, at work alongside her mother, a chambermaid and cleaning woman of the Columbus House Hotel—as swank a joint as Clyde Griffths' Kansas City hotel, the Green-Davison. Jennie is gazed upon, admiringly, by hotel guest Senator George Brander, struck by the girl's natural, and to him, flawless beauty.

In Jennie, who is "well-built," and "tall for a girl," we were in presence of a saint whose "goodness and mercy," Dreiser prologued, "had molded her every impulse." (Editing of the text excised Jennie's sexual urges—pg. 121, JENNIE GERHARDT, New Essays on the Restored Text, Ed. Hames L.W. West III). Maybe another Carrie Meeber too—emotional genius? A free spirit in any case—though tethered by poverty and circumstances...

Senator Brander (brand's her) was a 52-year old bachelor, and a "fine man," Dreiser wrote, though "not any too heavy mentally." He made acquaintance of Jennie and mother as they come in and out his room.

The Senator was touched by stories he listened to of the Gerhardt's poverty and troubles. Resolving to help the family (and perhaps himself?) he sent gifts and money their way. Also secured the out-of-work father a job as night-watchman.

Admirable generosity, but was it Christian charity?

Lechery slithered in soon enough: Brander moving in for a hot kiss on innocent Jennie's flushed cheek. She happily receiving the attention—from so strong and virile a figure! But does not grasp the implication of the move: Was she too dumb? Too numb? Or only innocent, as Dreiser insisted?

Jennie's ever-lengthening visits to the Senator's room start tongue's waging at the Hotel Snoopington. The mother got wind of the scuttlebutt and put the ki-bosh to the daughter's room visits with the Senator. The Senator was disappointed, as Jennie. Brander made a call to the Gerhardt hacienda; he asked Jennie to consider going into Seminary for a few years—after or before he married her. The relationship remained chaste—but how long could that last?

Gerhardt Senior, as Dreiser's real-life father, an immigrant from Germany (though Lutheran not Catholic). He too an intolerant religious bigot.

The Senator become a frequent visitor to the home. Took Jennie out on carriage rides and for walks. Visits that set the tongues of Gerhardt's neighbors flapping. One such neighbor informed the old man, who had been kept in the dark as to the frequency of the Senator's visits and number of gifts Jennie and the mother received. He reacted badly to the info.

When confronted by the father, the Senator protested the insinuation of the fellow's accusatory tone. Claiming all intents innocent. Besides, he wanted to marry her. "I will decide who she marries," old Gerhardt replied.

The Senator bowed out, for the nonce.

The Gerhardt kids picked-up coal in the railroad yard. One day, because there was no coal lying about, Bass Gerhardt climbed up into a car and pitched coal down to the others. A cop pinched Bass, who fought the guardian of the law. Bass was brought to jail, bail set at $10.

The family no got, mir Gott. Jennie went to the Senator to borrow. He was glad to see her—a little too glad, perhaps; he took her in hand, and otherwise.

Cut to a commercial.

Bass was sprung from the pokey.

Senator Handy had to leave town for Washington D.C. to attend to political business. He told Jennie he would come for her after his trip and marry her. He lay $500 on her as gift/payment.

In Washington, the Senator contracted diphtheria and died.

Old Gerhardt was soon told the truth of Jennie's condition (in a family way). He flipped: ordered Jennie from the home. She took shelter in a rooming house room.

Dreiser knew of the ostracism Jennie felt. Same exclusion as he felt in childhood. The omniscient voice of the narrator spoke: "When we are cast 'out' we have still the companionship of all that is, Nature is not ungenerous. Its winds and stars are fellows within you…this vast truth will come home, not in phrases but as a feeling, a comfort, which is the last essence of knowledge…" How often had Dreiser applied the comfort of the thought to himself?

Gerhardt Senior quit, disgusted—the job secured him by the Senator—and left home for Youngstown looking for work. Bass, meanwhile, left for Cleveland hoping to make a new start in life.

Jennie soon followed Bass—also to start anew, leaving her six-month old daughter with the mother.

Soon, most of Jennie's $500 had been spent, and with a mortgage payment due on the house, anxiety within the family was heightened.

Jennie made the round of stores, seeking work, but like Carrie Meeber in first days in Chicago, met only rebuffs. Giving up on stores she tried houses and was given employment as maid by a Mrs.

Bracebridge, a “prepossessing brunette,” and “conventionally fashionable type.”

A week later Mrs. Gerhardt and children arrived in Cleveland—like Sarah Dreiser picking up and moving to Chicago for the children’s sake. “JENNIE is probably the most autobiographical of Dreiser’s fictions,” wrote Charles Shapiro (pg. 14, THEODORE DREISER, Our Bitter Patriot). “Most faithful picture of the Dreiser clan,” wrote Jerome Loving (pg. 201, Loving). Sarah and clan set-up house in a rental. The house become a den of self-sacrifice; Jennie, Bass, and even young George out working, pitching-in to support; the mother holding down the fort with smaller children attending school.

Mrs. Bracebridge (just what Jennie needed!) served Jennie as Mrs. Hale and Mrs. Vance, two other conventional doyens of fashion, served Carrie Meeber. Jennie was clued-in as to matters of taste and decorum.

Meanwhile, Christmas time coming, old Gerhardt, the Torquemada of the family, decided to join the rest in Cleveland. He arrived in ignorance of the new baby, not knowing of new developments—out of the loop in Youngstown. His meeting with the daughter of concupiscence was frosty, but he too, as others, was taken with the lovely child.

Into the Bracebridge residence come Lester Kane, friend of the family, from Cincinnati; the son of a wealthy wholesale carriage-builder. 36-years old, “fine,” and “vigorous.”

“An unsuccessful imitation of Senator Brander” (pg. 23, Shapiro).

He took an instant shine to Jennie. Approaching her: “You belong to me,” he said. He forced a kiss on her—a cheeky riposte leaving Jennie indecisive and shaken—as well it might! An assault on a servant girl. By an “animal-man,” Dreiser wrote, “veneered by education and environment.”

Later, Lester insisted Jennie allow him to give her a lift home in his carriage. Once ensconced, he said, again, “You are mine.” And “I will have you," and "come!" Jennie protesting his advances—but not enough! She acting like a will-less automaton. She cannot, evidently, help herself; she yields to his embrace—but refused to take the money he offered. Quite a boy, Lester! Like a force of nature. A lightning bolt. Meteor…

The Kane's were well-placed in the world: big house, social distinction. Lester one of five Kane children. Good looking kids. Smart kids—future MENSA candidates perhaps. The mother refined, self-effacing. The father, Archibald, a "big man" and "honest man," come to wealth by fulfilling a need (transportation) not through inheritance. A self-made "good" man—sort of another Samuel Griffths, Clyde's rich Uncle, of Lycurgus N.Y.; he also with handsome smart children and refined wife.

A letter from old Gerhardt in Youngstown—only no money with it, just note informing of an accidental burning and news of his imminent return to the home.

The extra expense of the old man and loss of his income putting the family behind the 8-ball. Jennie thought of the money Lester had offered and she had refused; she decided to accept.

Lester slipped her $250. He also offered to set her and family up in a house. Jennie hesitated, worrying of the father's reaction. Lester wanted her to live with him: He is persuasive. She said she could not have a baby. He said she would not—though not specifying how that would be avoided.

A plan was worked-out: Jennie told the folks she was going on a trip with Mrs. Bracebridge.

Jennie failing to tell Lester she had a child. Returning home, Jennie clued her mother in on the plan. At the appointed time she met Lester and absconded with him—as his "niece."

For 3-years Jennie was a kept-woman. Living at home with the family except when with Lester elsewhere. Not in Cincinnati though: Lester staying away from the old home town...A secret relationship—the kid a secret too (to Lester). When he had to go to Chicago on business he called Jennie to the city. The Gerhardt household broke-up: two youngsters in school stayed with the old man; Vesta, the baby, was boarded with a nurse living nearby Chicago; Bass, Martha, and George had already left the home.

Lester finally discovering baby Vesta's existence. He deciding to stay with Jennie but also that he cannot now marry her (something he should have done already?).

One day Lester's sister dropped by and got an eyeful of the domestic situation. Old Man Kane dispatched elder son Robert to "confer" with Lester. Robert asked what Lester's plan regarding the ménage? Lester did not know; could not have said. Lester slowly becoming estranged from his family.

Lester buying a house in Hyde Park and he, Jennie, Vesta, and old man Gerhardt occupying the place. Vesta pawned-off as child of Jennie's deceased husband; Lester now the stepfather. A fantasy-past soon enough riddled with holes by snobbish biddies of Hyde Park's social hierarchy, descended like vultures upon "Mrs. Lester Kane." Lester's family meanwhile, distressed beyond measure—over the son's taking-up with a girl without money or pedigree—a "woman of the street."

Lester failing to show up at his sister's wedding: The family begun maneuvering Lester out the family business. Lester, arriving in Cincinnati for a showdown, is advised to either marry Jennie or leave her. If he did marry however, he was out of the old man's will; and if he left, the girl would be taken care of and he would be back in the fold.

Poor Lester. His society friends cutting him off; business associates giving him a cold shoulder; newspapers featuring the affair between the rich man's son and the servant girl.

Time passed. Lester made no decision (must be a Libra). He and Jennie took a trip to Europe: there Lester met an old flame of his earlier Cincinnati days, one Letty Pace—beautiful, rich, and newly widowed. Letty and Lester become chummy again—she the pursuer now, with her "I must have you," and Lester the pursued. Jennie did not intervene; stood by instead, brooding; thinking of what an attractive couple Lester and Letty made; thinking they should probably be together; thinking melancholic thoughts—

Eldest brother Robert Kane, cold fish of a businessman, merged the family business with a half dozen competitors, forming a giant trust, putting Lester further outside the family circle—further jeopardizing his inheritance.

Robert sent a lawyer to Jennie hoping she would bring Lester to his senses (and a return to the fold). Jennie advised of a substantial remuneration should she leave Lester.

Lester felt the increased pressure to decide. Would he crack? Throw his love away for filthy lucre? He tried a number of business ventures on his own but failed to make much of a score. Letty Pace awaited him in the wings. Time was running out on our Lester. A million and a half dollars awaiting his decision.

He accepted terms of his brothers, and his father's will. Back into the saddle. With Letty as new wife.

Jennie moving out the home and to Sandwood and a cottage on a lake. Once there, Vesta, poor girl, contracting typhoid and dying. The tragedy continuing when Lester—not so happy a camper apparently after leaving Jennie—eating and drinking himself into illness—expired via brain hemorrhage (calling Jennie not Letty to his bedside).

Did Lester truly love Jennie? Loved like the conqueror loved his conquest. Jennie's love the greater, seems to me. Greater sacrifice in her insistence Lester leave her for Letty and his inheritance. Should she have engaged a lawyer and took her rich consort to court? She would not do that, for, as Dreiser wrote, Jennie was born "to yield, not seek."

At end of story she sunk into melancholic reverie, her future marked by Dreiser by a question mark.

I DREAM OF JENNIE

Within a year of publication, JENNIE sold 12,000 copies (pg. 82, Lehan). Reviews of the novel were generally positive, and unlike CARRIE, carried by all major publications. Similarities to other novels included Edith Warton's HOUSE OF MIRTH, Zola's NANA, Hardy's TESS OF THE D'URBERVILLES, and, by H. L. Mencken, Hawthorne's THE SCARLET LETTER (a book Dreiser recalled, in DAWN, borrowing from the library as a schoolboy). Mencken's review of JENNIE included: "the best American novel I have ever read with the lonesome but Himalayan exception of HUCKLEBERRY FINN" (pg. 42, Lingeman, vol. 2).

Dreiser wrote Mencken that immediately after finishing JENNIE he wrote a draft of a new novel, THE GENIUS, and begun a 4th novel, THE FINANCIER.

Theo moved into the apartment of patrons of the arts Elias and Emma Rosenfeld (and begun an affair with their daughter). Theo also, at this time, met Sinclair Lewis and Emma Goldman (with whom Dreiser talked anarchism).

CONTINENTAL BREAKFAST

In 1907 Dreiser had been contacted by English publisher Grant Richards—who had corresponded with Dreiser since 1905 (pg. 805, Historical Commentary, A TRAVELER AT FORTY). In 1912 Dreiser met with Richards; he complained about a lack of money—money needed to research the life of his protagonist Frank Cowperwood of his novel-in-progress THE FINANCIER. Richard's sold Dreiser on making a deal with The Century Company, and their magazine The Century, for an up-front payment of $3000—for a travel book and 3-articles resulting from the book. Richard's also inveigled Dreiser to ask his American publisher for funds. To Dreiser's surprise, Harper & Brothers coughed-up an additional $3,000

In November, 1912, Dreiser sailed, with Richard's aboard, NYC to London, England. Richard's would serve as host and guide to Dreiser's projected continental trip. Richard's did have ulterior motives: hoping Dreiser would sign over THE FINANCIER to him—a novel already slated for Harper & Brothers.

Dreiser's opinion of the English was balanced through his knowledge of Americans. Comparison and contrasting. Certain English persons he disliked: the "too solid, too rosey, too immobile" ones; too "assured and stare-y." Also disliked what he called the English "race pride," remarking of Richard's "strong sense of individual and racial superiority."

From London Dreiser moved on to Paris. The parsimonious Dreiser worrying constantly about money—who would not be parsimonious after a childhood of dreadful poverty? A trait that irritated Richards who had known no such circumstances and so had little understanding of Dreiser's inferiority and insecurities. After hearing first sales reports on JENNIE Dreiser considered a return to the U.S, and maybe a return to his old job with Butterick (if they would have him!). Richard's persuaded him otherwise.

From Paris, Dreiser, Richards, and art dealer Hugh Lane visited the French Riviera; from there Dreiser roamed solo through Italy and into Germany. During a visit to his father's hometown of Mayen Theo was shocked when reading, on a gravestone, THEODOR DREISER GEB'N 16 FEB 1820 GEST'N 28 FEB 1882 (pg. 57, Lingeman, vol. 2). From Germany, back to London, where he attempted to buy a ticket on the Titanic, but made a last minute decision for a cheaper vessel!

Dreiser's account of his continental trip, published as A TRAVELER AT FORTY (1913) was published by The Century Publishing Co., after Harper & Brothers brought out THE FINANCIER (1912), first volume of Dreiser's TRILOGY OF DESIRE (a title "leaning heavily on Spencerian terminology"—pg. 82, James L.W. West III).

After JENNIE Dreiser said he was done with writing about women and would be writing about men in his next novels. In THE FINANCIER he chose, as subject, the American tycoon Charles T. Yerkes, an arrogant financial buccaneer of the Gilded Age in America—a man who strove only to satisfy himself.

THE FINANCIER

Frank Algernon Cowperwood: born in Philadelphia, Pennsylvania; two parents, three siblings. Father rose from bank clerk to cashier. A sturdy youth Frank, innately courageous and defiant. "Normal" but preternaturally bright, ambitious. Made his first money reselling soap, bought at a wholesale auction, to a shoe merchant. A financier at thirteen! Selling newspapers, shoes; forming other boys into a union...No scholar in school, but...so what? Rich Uncle Seneca got Frank a job in a grain and commission house. The youthful Nero shone; was a wiz, a keeper—but had higher ambitions and quit the house, entering employ of a brokerage firm. 18-years old, and saving money to invest in railroad transportation—street cars; it was a boon-time for street traffic in American cities.

Frank dreamt of becoming a "real man"—a creator; a leader; a financier.

Our Frank was a bit of a brooder too, like Carrie Meeber and Jennie Gerhardt, and like young Frank's love interest, Lillian Semple nee Wiggins, 5-years his senior, and married to owner of a shoe store (who died of pneumonia, poor guy—conveniently for the plot).

Uncle Seneca died too, leaving Frank $15,000 buckaroos. Just in time too, as the country on verge of a civil war (1860) and real money tight and tighter, hard to come by; stocks depreciating at an alarming rate, though Frank's streetcar stocks were rising, and his estate holdings holding their own—good to mortgage for ready cash, as needed.

Lillian's "lymphatic" body attracted Frank. "Like a figure on an antique vase out of a Greek chorus," Dreiser wrote. Frank attacked her one night, throwing her down, wrestling her onto the bed, she becoming aroused. It was her first rape: the ex-hubby non-rapist a dull passionless guy, unlike Frank.

Cowperwood agreed to a church wedding, but unenthusiastically. He not big on religion: Ten Commandments not his bag. The couple lived in Lillian's house which Frank and an architect re-did. Frank had notions of artistic refinement. Where he got the notions was anyone's guess. He no Philistine in taste. He saw examples of "fine art" on lawns and gardens of the rich; in interiors of well-to-do Philadelphian's homes; plus, the architect, recently graduated college, gave Frank some pointers.

A maid and man-of-all-work was installed. Frank come home from work to a wife-y wearing a "trailing gown of pale-blue or green silk." Lit candles on the supper-table.

In such coziness, kids inevitably followed; two of them, two years apart, squealing to life.

Cowperwood, or Cowperwood & Co., was contacted by Edward Butler, a contract man and political boss prospecting for street car lines. Ed and Frank agreeing to do business. While at Butler's home, Frank getting an eyeful of Butler's beautiful 18-year old daughter, Aileen.

Butler had friends in high places; Frank had the right contacts; a new bond issue was addressed, by Frank, to the tune of a cool million dollars; the deal putting Frank into the big-time; he becoming a known commodity. He met the governor of the state, plus assorted muckety-mucks.

With influx of funds, Frank built a new house; his father, now a bank President, built another alongside Frank. Meanwhile, Cowperwood frau, age thirty-two, to Frank's twenty-seven, was looking a little dragged-out, peaked—after two kids, and whatnot: a little fatigue. Frank started casting an eye about, scoping-out, in particular, Butler's luscious daughter. A healthy vivid and vital girl, schooled by nuns and priests, but never buying into Catholic doctrine. She hot to trot: cannot help herself—being who and what she is—how constituted (like Frank!). Fading Lillian took an instant dislike to the girl (business having brought the two families in proximity).

Mir Gott! The business machinations, political ramifications, personal shenanigans of those involved in financial-political rigmarole of the big city! Hard to follow descriptions of financial abstrusities. Not for Frank however: "The abstrusities of the stock exchange were as his ABC's," Dreiser wrote.

Par values, bonds and loans, securities, stock-gambling, pyramiding, kiting, wash sales, bulls and bears, hypothecation, defalection, warrants and reserve issues (I do not have a business degree, only a BA in Liberal Arts. Frank Cowperwood had no degree either, but unlike me, he a financial genius.)

Frank made a bundle on his dealings facilitated by city government (and state)—with the treasurer's connivance. Dealings not entirely illegal, but close...Nothing Standard Oil Company would not do in the years ahead.

Years passed: Frank is now a business address; his HQ an elaborate set-up: early Roman, nouveau riche Americano décor—early Florentine window dressing. Reserved and tasteful—"solid," and "assuring."

Cowperwood did not drink alcohol or smoke tobacco. He was a metal-minded accountant and an early riser who got the bid—and girl.

Dreiser took great pains in description of financial rigmarole as well as architecture of offices, homes, of Cowperwood & Co. In telling of new homes and gardens he reached descriptive apotheosis, piling in detail enough to overflow a landfill (a plethora H. L. Mencken complained of in his review of the novel).

Dreiser answered the mystery of Frank's artistic preciosity as critic, collector, and connoisseur: all intuitive. Born that way (and "finance" an art, he would have us believe). Like Carrie's "emotional genius"—innate, inbred—not learned on a farm or from the parental Philistines or an MFA program. Just one of those things, waiting to blossom under right circumstances...The architect is the font behind the refinements, but taste? Intuitive also?

Dreiser's years editing a woman's fashion magazine—The Deliniator—held him in good stead in describing outfits of his female characters. Like Aileen Butler's costume, worn to Cowperwood's open-house: "dark silk dress with velvet pelisse—trimmed with pleatings and shirrings." Her red-gold hair arranged in an enormous "chignon." Her sister Nora in a "pale lavender and white silk" number, "with fluffy hoop-skirt of daiaty lace—edged ruffles." Aileen's nighttime costume killed them all: "black satin, glistening crimsoned silver sequins—low-cut corsage receding back and front into a deep V...draped overskirt of black tulle and silver tissue..."

Cowperwood sidled up and in a poetic moment, words come unbidden from his lips, spoke into Aileen's ear: "you're like fire and song."

Frank's name getting put on Aileen's dance-card. "You're darling. I am afraid of you," he whispered, shooting her an "interpretive" glance.

Her bosom heaved.

"You like me?" he asked. She thrilled at the question. "A piece of ice," Dreiser commented, "dropped down her back could not have startled her more."

Mrs. Cowperwood grew older-looking as Frank watched Aileen. Frank knew he was treading on thin ice by attentions to a mere girl. But why, he wondered, shouldn't he tread? What was it anyway about one person clinging to another for a lifetime? Cleaving "until death" even, though perhaps one or both not wanting to? He disliking the idea: moral straight-jacketing upheld by cant and hypocrisy. He would serve his own moral or amoral nature, he thought—daring those who would condemn to do so. He would satisfy himself. "I satisfy myself," his new motto.

Reflecting on his wife, Frank thought of the "cold purity of (a) snowdrift" in combination of her "murky mood(s) of the wonton"—ashamed she was of the passion that sometimes came over her. Though dutiful, Frank thought, she was essentially passionless. Unlike Aileen.

And yet—

And yet, nothing: he planted a kiss on Aileen while she sat at a piano playing Schubert. The cat was out the bag.

In grip of a "chemic-connection" Aileen could not help reacting. Dreiser had put forth a theory in JENNIE on "chemism"—the mysterious effect occurring between persons. He had wrote of ketabases and anabases as instrumental in drawing people together—the basis of attraction. Was it so? Aileen "put her lips to his and dreamed into his eyes." That's chemism. The two become lovers, chemically and otherwise connected. Frank arranging liaisons, and knowing, Dreiser informed, how to avoid complications (as in "interruptus" like Theo? Or is he, Frank, a man for "reservatus"?) The trysts happening at a love nest Frank rented.

In the meantime, Frank cleaned-up on stock market speculations. Making big money for his father and two brothers as well. Did spread himself a little thin however, with so many irons in the fire—on way to consolidation, he hoped, of various street car lines. Picking up the pace too with his collection of rugs, china, porcelain, statues, and paintings—bringing in experts to confer with over each genre.

Frank felt good about things in general: his wealth, health; living high on the hog; but—in 1871, got knocked down a notch or two when the Great Chicago fire of that year caused a financial panic that meant, in Philadelphia and elsewhere, withdrawal of deposits, calling-in of loans, and depression of securities. Frank sat on the hot seat. Would he go to ruin? He worried about his involvement, via a scheme of dubious legality, with city and state treasurers to the tune of half-a-million dollars. How to explain should the transactions come to light? Could mean his ruin; ruin of the Republican Party too, through defeat in the next election. A defeat putting the kibosh on wheeler-dealers like Frank avidly benefitting through political associations.

Things become exciting in the financial world. The machinations not entirely understood (by me) but exciting still—like excitement Frank Norris built up in his novel of the Chicago stock-market, THE PIT. What was understood was that Frank was in a pickle because not enough ready cash to pay-off loans being called-in.

Needing help—on the verge of failure—Frank went to Edward Butler, Aileen's father, who in turn, went to Mollenhauer, old lion of finance, who called on Senator Simpson. These three power brokers pow-wow, each lying through clenched-teeth approximating smiles. Would they join to help rescue Cowperwood? And thereby themselves, from the coming tide driven by the next panic?

Insurance company's unable meeting obligations were calling-in all loans to save themselves. Cowperwood needed finagle another $350,000 out of Sterner, city treasurer, partner in duplicity, to hold-out, staving off creditors. Sterner however, was under threat of fierce Mollenhauer (who had placed Sterner in the job).

Turning the heat up on Frank was Butler, who had discovered his daughter stepping out with 34-year old married Frank. Butler, previously so friendly to Frank. Old Butler's hurt was tragic, the story pulling at heartstrings—which was Dreiser's real subject—and his greatness. Particularly concerning Butler, the outraged parent hurt beyond measure by Aileen throwing her life away possibly, through such dalliance. Butler vowing to drive Cowperwood out of the city.

Frank was forced to shut-down his brokerage house. The "Municiple Reform association"—a group of city watch dogs—publicly called Frank out for his "vicious" financial practices (to wit: manipulation of cash and securities belonging to the city, for personal gain). A smear of Frank by powerbrokers Butler, Mollenhaur, and Simpson ensuing. Leading to indictment of Cowperwood for embezzlement and larceny.

Frank, a cool cat, unbothered however, or appearing so; conscienceless—unconcerned with "sin" or even right and wrong. Amoral. Though open to a "higher power"—or Emerson's 'oversoul' (Dreiser big on Emerson as on Thoreau) a ruling something, but believing, essentially, only in himself; his power, magnetism, intelligence, strength, which would, he thought, win the day—any day. Moved by courage and energy. A brave philosophy, but how well would it work?

Butler the rugged old ward boss become financier had a hard-on for Frank. Butler engaged services of the Pinkerton Agency to tail Frank and daughter Aileen to the house of assignation. Butler thought violence appropriate as response but settled for spiriting Aileen away from wolfish Frank.

Cowperwood went to trial. The judge was Judge Payderson (payback), the court bailiff "Sparkheaver," and the clerk "Mr. Profus." Description of the trial somewhat lengthy (like this synopsis) and tedious reading—not as long as the trial of Dreiser's TRAGEDY (not nearly as long or tedious as the trial at end of Dostoevsky's THE BROTHERS KARAZAMOV).

Ill-gotten gains of Frank playing too loose with poorly supervised freedoms of his position.

He was sent to Moyamensing Prison—County jail. Given special privileges as a convict of means. (American poet Charles Bukowski spent 17-days in the prison in mid-1940, for failing to register for the draft).

Meanwhile, at the Butler residence, Aileen packed her bags, departing to a friend's home. She would not drop Cowperwood nor go to Europe, as her father wished. She loved Frank and would stay by him she vowed until he was able to marry her—as he said he would.

Frank was let out of prison for an interim period, before reporting to do a 4-year stretch. Butler showed up at Frank's house, super-pissed. Frank was suave, though a little greasy (it seemed)—despite Dreiser's attempt to keep him personally pristine. The old ward boss was no match for Frank's brand of sophistry (lying).

Frank's co-conspirator, the city treasurer, received a 4-year sentence also.

Frank exchanged his silk suit for convict garb: striped pants and shirt, clogs, hat plus hood that covered the convict's faces as they walked. A real prison prison. Inhuman. Inhumane. Each of the 400-convicts kept to separate cells. All set to working, alone. Frank making cane-bottomed chairs. The prison pocketing the fruits of convict labor. For a price, a guard made Frank's prison life less monastic: Frank's business partner regularly visiting as did his lawyer; Aileen was allowed in as were Frank's wife, children, and father (bank clerk again, instead of President).

Frank did 13-months in the slammer. Let out after death of old Butler (who had fought against a pardon).

6-months after sprung from the joint, the financial panic of 1873 erupted, initiated by the failure of the banking house of Jay Cooke & Co. Frank made a cool million in the crash, enough to exit the City of Brotherly Love for the "west,"—meaning Chicago, the Windy City, City of the Broad Shoulders, Chi, Ciberia, Hog-Butcher of the World; that toddlin' town; home to Studs Lonigan, Bigger Thomas, Jadwin Curtis, Augie March, and other notables (James T. Farrell, Richard Wright, Frank Norris, Saul Bellow).

TITANIC TEDDY

Sales of THE FINANCIER, despite a fast start of 8,000 sold copies (pg. 167, Swanberg) tailed off, and in the 2nd year sold only 2,000 copies (pg. 83, Lingeman, vol. 2).

While visiting Chicago to do research for his proposed next novel THE TITAN, Dreiser become involved with The Little Theater crowd, including introduction to Margaret Anderson (future editor of "The Little Review"), poet/lawyer Edgar Lee Masters—whom Dreiser formed a life-long friendship with; and actress Kirah Markham (18-years old to Dreiser's forty) who moved to NYC to continue an affair with Theo (though he still involved with wife, Jug). Dreiser also met, in this period, Sherwood Anderson, still writing advertising copy, and John Cowper Powys, the English mystic and literary critic. (Also spending time with Hamlin Garland, discussing Philistines—pg. 186, Swanberg).

Due to involvement with the theater Dreiser turned to writing drama (had originally fashioned himself a playwright). Mostly short plays, some of which were produced—all of which published. One full-length play—much praised, much scorned—"The Hand of the Potter" dealing with sexual perversion and murder.

Dreiser also, in this period, wrote one of his best short stories, "The Lost Phoebe," featuring Henry Reifsneider and wife Phoebe Ann—living together on a dilapidated homestead, their children long scattered to the wind. Phoebe Ann died in the 48th year of the marriage; the husband lost his mind, and went out daily and nightly in search of his wife. His derangement obvious, but authorities letting him alone, neither stopping nor confining him—becoming a "character" to the country folk, and likewise tolerated.

One night the old man saw his wife; she dancing in a wind, her eyes like fire flies; he followed her perceived form, went over a cliff and died.

"A deluded quest for the unobtainable," Richard Lingeman wrote (pg. 72, vol. 2).

"Dreiser's most poetic story," F.O. Matthiesson commented (pg. 121, Shapiro).

TRAVELING MAN

As mentioned earlier, Dreiser took a trip to England and the continent in 1907, through the largesse of English publisher Grant Richards. The travelogue Dreiser wrote telling of his trip would be published by the Century Publishing Co. in 1913.

A TRAVELER AT FORTY

Off the dock, and over the "noble but unendurable" sea (whose motions sickened him) went Theodore Dreiser, with a $1500 advance from The Century Magazine and a promise of $2500 more from the The Century Publishing Co. on delivery of a "travel book." (Another $3,000 supplied by his American publisher Harper & Brothers.)

Crossing over, arriving in old England, Dreiser—as was his wont, begun comparing English life and manner to American ("Amayreekan" as the English said), usually finding American things and people a bit better than their English counterparts. England's railroad cars seemed to Dreiser like toys, so much smaller and less powerful than the veritable iron-horses of American locomotion. People also, of England, more anemic-looking, without bustle and hustle of more forceful go-getting Americans. Far less vim and vigor.

English countryside and rural villages were charming, Dreiser thought—like pastoral poems; and the English rural character sweet and romantic, and of a certain pathos.

English servants had it over their American counterparts in spades our man from Indiana reported. The English servants Dreiser observed seemed to like their jobs—were happily, even warmly, eager to assist the needy. Glad to be of service. A temperamental difference between servants of the two nations. Unlike their American facsimiles the English servants were "civil," "wise"; they called out quietly and pleadingly, not brash, loud, irritably; English servants more considerate, human: one was not "driven," not made to feel merely tolerated (as in America). Indeed, "rauther" helped along.

Dreiser was good at mimicking English speech: Grant Richards said "you won't see the same thing hyah that you do in America.

Ovah babashops are less imposing. Hyah we do it quickly—get it ovah with."

Richards' gardener: "most extrawdinary."

A cockney: "'ere you are, loidy...Foine potitoes these are, Madam, hextra nice."

A servant: "I might harsk if you're hanxious to know."

London was a treat for our man from Terre Haute, but wearying too—"a city two to four stories in height stretching away in endless reaches of drab grays and yellows." An "uncharted sea," Dreiser concluded, no one person could thoroughly know. Streets narrow and drab, houses tasteless and uniformly dull.

He was introduced to modern art—post-Impressionism. At first glance did not think much of it, his idea of art being the picturesque: correct drawing, artistically arranged, harmonizing colors...An idea he revised warming to the work, standing before van Gogh, Gauguin, Cezanne, and others. He decided both representational and non-representational work to have equal value, liking or disliking either a matter of temperament.

Dreiser remarked on the absence of electric lighting of London at night. Where was the light? The mega-wattage of American cities like New York, Chicago, Boston? It was a shocking even frightening experience for an American introduced to London or Dublin at night (I know).

Per arrangement, Theo was shuffled around London to soirees of one type and another: theater, museum, concert, dinner...In his open-minded ex-country boy manner, Dreiser, always ready to be awed, made comment on each experience, comparing, contrasting, with similar or relatable of his American experiences. The weighing of these experiences usually heavier on American ones. England he found deficient in vitality possessed by Americans; deficient too in creative imagination (though English countryside "idyllically charming"). He also stated that the U.S. had had far more influence on English-life than vice-versa. A statement, openly spoken, raising a bit of a contretemps, sometimes vituperative. On Londoners, he remarked: "solid, hard, phlegmatic; a little dreary"—with certain attitudes of "drab acceptance of the commonplace" predominating.

Everyone becomes lonely—even a giant like Dreiser—despite his new celebrity status and new "society" friends. He picked-up a Welsh tart on the street and sympathized with her circumstances, feeling the pathos of her existence. After treating her shabbily though, he become civil, taking her to lunch and afterward buying her gifts. He interviewed her as to her trade, eliciting a very "human" story of woe. The girl, aged nineteen, had soft eyes, thought Theo—not mean enough, he thought, for her to really succeed at her trade. The two toured the London demimondaine as couple.

Did he sleep with her? He did not say.

The travelogue most un-Baedeker, even anti-Baedeker. Full of personal as well as poetic impressions of English landscape, cityscape, weather, humankind...Baedeker with a soul.

Our Theo went gaga over Oxford, with its twenty-two colleges, halls, churches, museums, and the like. Without a high school diploma, and with one desultory year of University, Dreiser talked architecture with experts; art with artists; opera with aficionados of the genre...An exemplary auto didactical personage, our Theo.

Dreiser become friendly with a friend of Grant Richards', Hugh Lane, artist and architect. Huge showed Dreiser a Frans Hals and a Rembrant he kept in his apartment. Dreiser bowed down to the two Dutchmen (as van Gogh once did, when in Amsterdam). Lane and his friends, including George Moore and John Sergeant, were decidedly academic in taste, abhorring the new art of neo-Impressionism as expressed in works of van Gogh, Gauguin, Cezanne, et al. Dreiser however, saw the new work as tonic in its reaction against "spindling over-refinement" and come to belief that neo or post-Impressionism heralded a return to artistic force and sanity. Smart man! (He did however wrongly attribute Gauguin's "Yellow Christ" to van Gogh.)

Theo visited Manchester, industrial center of England. The day dark, gloomy, "lowery," Dreiser wrote, but found poetry in contrasting light and dark chiaroscuro, and in mist over the river, and great blocks of factories he called "vast temples of labor," whose windows "gleamed in the smoke and rain." All more impressive, he thought, than the factory-scenes of Fall River or Lawrence, Massachusetts.

His trip to the sooty region one more of his explorations, in prose, of the potentiality of beauty in ugliness.

PLASTER OF PARIS

Dreiser become rapturous in descriptions Parisian. “Even London,” he wrote, “a dreary horror after Paris.” Such gay vital people in the French capital! Like Americans for hustle and bustle; and without America’s god-awful Puritanical streak. Without those prudish guardians of morals. Parisians unlike the more staid, quiet, and home-y English. Music in the air of Paris and a thrilling sense of life, like nowhere else our man from the American mid-West and New York had ever encountered in his well-traveled life.

The snap and intensity of the Parisians—their emotions, ambitions, and romances—only in America could be found the equal for child-y enthusiasm, effervescence, sharpness of dress, and uninhibited savoir faire. The ou la la perhaps. (But all a kind of subterfuge, he also thought—a kind of dumb show, disguising s-e-x.) Dreiser reveled in the show but looked through appearances, and wrote a scathing passage on desire in the Montmartre district of Paris: “consumption, cocaine, and opium maintains their persistent toll. This furnace of desire burns furiously with a hard, white-hot flame until there is nothing left save black cinders and white ashes. Enduring the consuming heat renders emotion and feeling and beauty no more.”

Whenever on his own, roaming, cities or waterways, Dreiser often begun to sound, on the page, like a Baedeker guide, or worse, like a Chamber of Commerce tourist brochure. His repetitions multiplied in use of similar phrases and words in descriptions of whatever caught his fancy or stirred enthusiasm. It is when with others, his account—his travelogue—shone brighter. Others added a humanity, absent in much landscape and cityscape reiteration. Though scenes rendered poetically, the rendering become tiring in similar multiplication. Luckily, for the book, and reader, there are others: Grant Richards and family, Hugh

Lane, strangers Dreiser befriends, the Welsh rarebit Mary, landlords, clerks, policemen, who come and go throughout the narrative.

Grant Richards returned to Paris, after a week away from the city and Dreiser. Richards had in tow four others: Hugh Lane, Arthur Calvin (museum curator), Mr. Flexon (writing a study of prostitution), and an American publisher. Theo and company went out for a night on the town, seeking particularly sordid nightlife. Dreiser not adverse to sordidness (interested in life of all forms). Richards however, dismissive of all to do with "smut." Aesthetics his branch of pleasure, though like Theo, also a lady's man.

The trio of Richards, Dreiser, and Hugh Lane left Paris for Marseilles and hence along the coast toward Monte Carlo and the Riviera.

Dreiser's accounting of the trio along the Cote d'Azur contained some skewering of both Richards and Lane; the humor of the accounting—scathingly funny—worthy of a Celine. While Dreiser was not known as a humorist, he could be howling funny at times—this Monte Carlo adventure one of the times (other times found in his short stories "The Cruise of the Idlewild," and "Phantom Gold.").

Lane made to appear curmudgeonly misogynistic and Richards conniving and dialectical; Dreiser rube-like and willingly following like a jackass, kicking or balking—as the mood struck him—at his more sophisticated and experienced confreres.

Great fun!

Dreiser alone, with his propensity for brooding introspective rumination was bad company; with others he was often delightful (depending of course on who the others), playing the drudge, clown, foil, or even Man of the World—as circumstance warranted.

Exchanges between Dreiser and Richards almost always amused. Lane rode Richards unmercifully over his, Richards, "gormadizing." Lane is like a Savonarola, contemning the other two for their multiple dalliances. Theo with a French "cocotte;" elle ne parle pas English.

WHEN IN ROME

Dreiser headed east, into Italy, by his lonesome. In Pisa, he rose to panegyric: "buildings finer than anything in Rome," or Venice, or Florence, or London—"noble, beautiful things."

After some Baedeker-like rhapsodies, Theo riffed into very Dreiserian ruminations on fate and destiny.

Theo looked-up Grant Richards' mother ("Grawntie" to his ma) in Rome. Soon Theo calling the woman "ma," or "mum," as well.

Accumulative piles of details in Dreiser's novels added to overall sense of time and place, but in a travelogue become senseless. For instance, the church of St. Peter, Dreiser related, contained 46-altars, 748-marble columns, 386-statues, and 290-windows. Did anyone care about such minutia? Enough of piling, and senselessness threatened. The churches added up. He is shown a piece of the original cross; a patch of dirt from Gethsemane; a piece of the robe worn by Hayzeus Christy…While in company of an American woman, one Mrs. Armstrong (what a moniker) who is newly separated from a husband—and too worried about being watched to favor Theo.

She is big on the Borgias—their incestuous and murderous years of rule (worse than the Kardashians). Dreiser related to the whole bloody vain-glorious saga. Stuffing himself with Roman history, feasting ravenously then regurgitating onto the page like a gluttonous gourmand. While in sight of "faultless" architecture and "princely" grandeur—ilex and clumps of cypress adorning.

St. Paul Without Walls. Begun in 325 A.D. and completed in 388 A.D. 412-foot long, 216-foot wide; destroyed in an 1823 fire. The nave had 80-Corinthian columns in 4-rows; 40-portraits of Popes, above the columns…

The Armstrong woman declined to accompany our man to Assisi, Spello, or Perogia. Assisi brought on some portentous phlegmatic Dreiserian pondering on the nature of spirituality; humble Spello merely a pit-stop; Perugia "most remarkable, most sparkling" of all Italian hill-cities. Florence, or "Firenze," suggested, in its "compact, dark atmosphere," wrote Dreiser, Paris—as once was. Paris, along with Oxford, Pisa, Amiens, and Canterbury, the measuring rods of Dreiser's scale for beauty and grandeur.

Churches, museums, and the river (Arno); all were gawked. For paintings, Florentine museums were up there, Dreiser opined, with those of Paris and Rome.

All during this Italian idle our man of words had been strangely chaste—which changed when he met, on a train to Venice, a languorous German-Italian blonde; a "phlegmatic" type who spoke German (as did German-American Dreiser).

Venice! Light, airy, graceful, delicate! Theo was captured, soul and mind—like so many before him; his noted raptures turned poetical. Mari, of the train ride, lived in Venice, with her mother. Theo spent time at their apartment and his hotel flat. All told, the bill run him $65.

For five days the accounting becomes utterly human again. But Theo left Venice for Milan, returning clinically dissecting in comparison of earlier-visited Italian cities to those presently arrived at. (He is, though, he wrote, "sick" of art.)

Struck by the newness of Milan: newer-looking than Buffalo, New York, and department stores in Saint Louis and Philadelphia. Next he was in mountain land: Switzerland. Into "terrible, but real" beauty. Lucerne of craggy peaks, still lakes…

In Germany he met soldiers at every turn. Saw their aggressive displays as not at all ominous; he celebrating the pageantry of dress and drill and spit-shine while viewing their oftentimes announced "superiority" as but a national quirk. Never considering the blatant militarism and feeling of superiority only a few years later would cost millions their lives proving Germany not superior, and would not dominate others (only the war ended and armistice signed without allied armies marching into Germany. Defeated on the battlefield but her homeland still intact, twenty years later Germany remilitarized and begun bawling superiority again, and again, had to be defeated, and again, millions of lives—more than in the previous war—lost in proving Germany not superior and without right to dominate others).

Germans sat in pubs in Mayen, Theo's father's place of birth, looking like "animated potatoes" whenever speaking, Dreiser wrote. But such fine uniforms! So distinguished-looking (the officers)!

Frankfort, Germany, looked like Cleveland, Ohio, to Dreiser—same solid aggressive commercial aspect. People in the city looked like those in Cleveland: hustling, vital, striving forward, "as if they had something to strive for."

In Berlin Theo stayed at the home of Madame Culp, internationally recognized chanteuse. Married, but had designs on Grant Richards, and tried to fit Theo in too, to her romantic proclivities.

Berlin is better, to Theo; fresher, cleaner, than Paris or London, though he remarked disparagingly about city architecture, particularly the terrible Unter den Linden (German Reichstag building "beneath comtempt"). But saw good things as well, and decided the city like Chicago—a positive comparison…Also, again, impressed—awe-struck even, by the military demonstrations, precise, smart, thorough—never wondering where all the formidable display leading to (to Verdun, the Somme, Chateau Thierry…).

Another of the objectionable (to his English publisher) woman of the streets entered the narrative: Hanscha, an indifferent prostitute (working girl), not really hardened or mercenary enough, Dreiser thought, for success in the business. A "nice" girl in unfortunate circumstances.

Dreiser had a soft spot for such: the phlegmatic melancholy girl who drifted along letting life's flow take her: a Jenny Gerhardt type. The affair lasted a few days; he left with heavy heart, wondering why life had not been kinder to such girls as Hanscha.

Day of happy exit from Berlin arriving, Theo went to Holland—still dancing attendance on singing deva Madame Culp, though his hope for intimacy never panned-out. He gladly told her "au revoir," becoming anxious to end his trip. He had a happy encounter with Dutch art: Hals, Rembrant, Vermeer, Maes, de Hooch, Ruysdal, et al. Struck by the "kindly cleanly realism" of the work. Its delight in life and simplicity of living captured on the smooth painting surfaces.

Back in Paris the maestro met up with Grant Richards—after their two month separation. Richards his usual ebullient self. Dreiser in one of his phlegmatic moods, unhappily worried about the state of his finances and suspecting Richards of somehow deceiving him, mishandling his money, and leaving him to return broke to New York.

An offered walking-tour in the south of England was canceled by Theo. He wanted to go home. Now!

Our man from Amayeeka left Dover on his 10-day crossing of the "vastly suggestive, grimly poetic," gray-green waters. On his 4th day out word come over the wireless that the Titanic had sunk, ending the lives of 1500 passengers and crew.

POST MORTUM

TRAVELER come out, in Richard Lingeman's phrase, "an editorially battered child." Dreiser become involved in a tremendous row with The Century Company over content. Mostly related to the "women stuff," much of which Dreiser agreed to excise. More problems rising over possible libelous content. Another bone of contention thrown by Grant Richards objecting to his portrayal and that of his friends, and screaming for additional cuts (and at one point, threatening to sue Dreiser). Frank Doubleday-like, Richards did little to sell the book in England post-publication. (Interestingly, Richards had been against publication of McTEAGUE in England, delaying the book's appearance in that country for many years—pg. 4, FRANK NORRIS, A Life, Joseph R.M. Elrath Jr. and Jesse S. Crisler).

TRAVELER sold 2200 copies in the 2-months post-publication (pg. 170, Swanberg).

THE GOOD SHIP TITAN

Harper & Brothers, American publisher with contract to publish Dreiser's sequel to THE FINANCIER, had decided to hold back THE TITAN, avoiding The Century and Company's publication of TRAVELER. However: after moving to a first printing, Harper suddenly decided to pull the book (shade of SISTER CARRIE!). John Lane & Company, another English publisher, stepped in to publish. Lane gave Dreiser a $1000 advance and royalty of 20% (pg. 237, Loving).

In 1915 Dreiser moved to The Village, Greenwich Village, a New York City Bohemian enclave, then in its heyday. Kirah Markham joined him. Kirah reportedly loving Dreiser but refusing to stay with him for long because of his "varietism." Dreiser, reportedly, loved Kirah in return but doomed the relationship with incessant and self-destructive philandering. After Kirah left she aligned herself with the Provincetown Playhouse and took roles in Eugene O'Neill plays.

THE TITAN

Cowperwood walked into the office of Addison, one of the biggest bankers of Chicago. Addison was drawn to Cowperwood immediately. Why? Because, as Dreiser would have us believe, Frank exuded a kind of charisma—a certain force, or chemism, that turned people awe-stricken in his presence. He needed not to speak even; the force come out his eyes, gray-blue orbs suggesting…what? An inner something—greatness perhaps? Strength? He told Addison of his past, in Philadelphia; his 13-months in the penitentiary; his ex-wife and two children; his bankruptcy. Addison, who begun admiring Frank on first sighting, admired him even more after the confession. He could not do enough for Frank: become another Cowperwood worshiper. Like Aileen Butler, daughter of the late Edward Butler. Aileen who thought Cowperwood a god.

Frank visited an old financier named Peter Laughlin; he too bowled-over by Frank's aura of…indomitableness? Steadfastness? Solidity? Laughlin agreed to a partnership deal; was willing to accept 49% of the ownership even, leaving Frank in control at 51%. Laughlin a sort of "character"—lonely older man living with a dog—kind of a crackpot; the kind who took to Cowperwood like a duck to water.

Weakness bowing to strength.

Another character, Henry Sippens, come on board the Cowperwood. A failed financier, former gas-man, doing business on the fringes without connection to powerful city business cabals—those who shoved him aside in earlier years. He signed on to become manager in the realm of Frank—in process of becoming a powerhouse in the gas-business. Buying in with the help of Addison, Laughlin, and Sippens, and already scheming to consolidate his rival companies.

Addison steered Frank to a powerful city lawyer, a dusty old sinner named General Judson P. Van Sickle. The General was prosperous but not too much so—like Laughlin and Sippens. He also a character; wrinkled and unkempt, like General Grant. A phlegmatic disillusioned type, ready and willing to be used by a man of superior intelligence and life-force. A man like—

33-year old McKibben attracted Cowperwood due to an "agnostic unreadableness," and was retained to play on sympathies of certain councilmen Frank needed help from. Then Stimson, another lawyer, youthful Romeo, born poor and eager to succeed, agreeing to serve Frank, or even, Dreiser wrote, "kiss the arch-episcopal hand" of Cowperwood.

Like a wily General—Lee rather than Grant—Cowperwood sent his men to reconnoitering then surrounding the enemy—those opposing gas-companies, north, south, and west of the city.

After his rivals thrashed and the companies incorporated, Cowperwood decided to indulge his passion for art—or is it his passion for collecting? Art, women, money, whatever. A passion that spoke—as did the "varietism" of Dreiser's sexual life, of insecure men attempting to find security through possessions.

With Aileen, who at this point of the narrative, but an attractive adjunct and clothes-horse—non-spoken except in cooing and giggling, Frank boarded ship for Europe. In Paris he bought a Millet, a small Jan Steen, and a Gerome.

After Versailles and Fontainebleau he and wife returned to Chicago and the building of a mansion, French-styled, overseen by Frank's architect, Mr. Lord (how apropos). While waiting for completion of the house, the Cowperwoods strove to belong among the Chicago elite, for social recognition and equality if not supremacy. At least Aileen strove. Frank did not seem to care about society—though ambitious as a Mephistopheles for wealth. People sought Frank: his magnetism, Dreiser suggested, drawing them, those others, like moths to a light. Aileen however, did care; cared too much perhaps. She found social intercourse problematical. Never had she been a hostess previously—always cared for and petted by well-off parents. Never venturing far from the nest until arrival of Frank—like a comet—into her pampered life. She found the women of high society, of social distinction, intimidating and remote and nearly impossible to approach. The lesser, less distinct, socialites ended up filling her social calendar: Mrs. Sledd, for instance (easy sledding); Mrs. Cotton (cotton to Aileen's picking); and Mrs. Hoecksemas (nouveau riche Bohunk).

Many of the women were troubled by Aileen's showiness, referring to her as gauche, ostentatious...Like the nudes of Gerome Frank had hung on his wall (shocking to the uninitiated, but not the illuminati). Aileen seemed a bit of a social-climber to some. Too eager to impress. The jury remaining out as to the Cowperwood's acceptance into inner social circles.

On the business scene, Cowperwood who had had things pretty much his way of recent years, was challenged by one Schryhart (he grabbed the jugular), an old and proven Chicago hand, out for grabbing some of the gas profits flowing Frank's way. The shrewd Shredhart aimed to consolidate Frank's three rival gas companies. Frank seeking out John J McKenty, "patron saint of the social underworld of Chicago," to counter the thrust of Schryhart.

McKenty, analogous to Edward Butler of Philadelphia in affiliations, also found Cowperwood impressive—also stricken by Frank's personality—and willing to consider Frank's petition for help to defeat rival gas-men. So considered, McKenty agreed to go along with a Cowperwood scheme for consolidation. Frank's aggressive, and to his competitors, "scoundrel" actions (who had they opportunity would have acted likewise) created ill-feeling in the city toward the upstart Philadelphian. Schryhart in particular took his defeats at the hand of Frank bitterly, flaming a revolt against the Cowperwood's acceptance into Chicago high-society. Stories of Frank's previous incarceration and of Aileen's cheating-ways were exchanged, and the social opposition solidified. The Cowperwoods become social pariahs, a fallen state Aileen took to heart, her suffering acute—while Frank took his ostracism in stride, fancying becoming ever richer would dissolve the social bru-ha-ha in his favor eventually.

Out of the social defeat Frank come to belief Aileen had held him back. He met Rita, a semi-phlegmatic type, "unctuously full-bodied" wife of a violin-playing Dane. The husband nebulous. Inconsequential—"like a stormy, erratic boy."

Rita Solberg (soul-berg) was younger than Aileen, aged thirty-two, to Rita's twenty-seven. Rita, like Aileen, in "animality" but better, sweeter, more delicate; and richer spiritually (so thought Frank). A brainier more soulful Aileen.

The affair heated up like a flame to a dry pine bough. "You clover blossom," Frank said. "You sprig of cherry bloom. You Dresden china dream." Love made people say weird stuff. So did infatuation—and it appeared that was Frank's trip. It lasted though, a year or more, during which time the husband studied in Europe, where Rita followed—not to meet hubby but Frank (Alieen stayed home).

Rita advised Frank as to art purchases; she invigorated his taste buds. She an artistic siren Frank responded to.

In between Rita and Aileen, Frank was scoping-out his office secretary as well: Minka Nowak (real not stage name). A Polish pierogi whose father worked in a steel mill.

Minka took dictation (ha!) in the inner office as Cowperwood hovered, shooting glances between clauses, after run-on sentences, within ellipses...One day he took her hand and she yielded; one day he took more than her hand; one day she let it all go, caught like a baby seal in the arms of a polar bear.

A form of coercion; of abuse. Rape, even; the superior and underling, boss and secretary—an old saw. Would she have yielded so readily had Frank been janitor?

The serial-seduction world of Frank Harris related in his MY LIFE AND LOVES. Staring the variant Frank A. Cowperwood, whose conduct, discovered by his wife, brought accusations—blithely denied by Frank. Who had the gall—the effrontery—to say that even were he to cheat on her it would not mean he had been unfaithful spiritually (!).

Aileen scented detectives on Frank's tail. Through the dicks she come to knowledge of both Rita and Minka.

Cowperwood's trifling with the heart strings of his wife rebounding on him in fury. Aileen catching and beating lovely Rita to a pulp—a near murder. A frightened Cowperwood come upon the fight scene, jumping about like a grasshopper on a hot grill. A disgraceful and cowardly attempt to calm his wife further inflaming Aileen's passion. She throwing her jewels into his face while screaming that she hated him. She running out the house: he following, unable to let things go. Pleading with her not to leave. A ruse? Or did he actually have a heart?

Harold Solberg, musician and husband, was not so erratic or nebulous as not to suspect something untoward fueling Aileen's fit of "insanity" (as Frank labeled her act). After a show of bravado, Harold was cowed by both a threat to his life, made by Cowperwood, and a pay-off of $5,000 yearly in exchange for his silence. Aileen then returning to the house on condition Frank drop the secretary.

Cowperwood turned focus onto street car lines, north, south, and west divisions; securing the help of McKenty, the old fixer, Frank went to work, finagling his way to control of the North Chicago street car line, one of the big three city lines.

Meanwhile, Aileen, unhappy woman, brooding in her mansion. Gave all to Cowperwood, and lost all. The light she made her own, burnt-out;

now she in the dark. Like an old suit, still wearable, but never worn; she sat in her gorgeous castle with a husband whose politeness and gallantry substituted for real love.

Stephanie Platlow entered, with her "interesting variability of soul" and a "fulgurous gleam" in brownish-black eyes. Another sensuous, artistic-type, in the mold of Rita Soulberg. Why these young (Steph is twenty) lithe artistic chicks went for inartistic stolid commercially-minded burgher Frank was somewhat a mystery.

Stephanie, like Rita, had not needed Frank's money, her father being wealthy. Stephanie acted in amateur dramatic productions. Aileen liked Stephanie—inviting her to the house. Frank noticed Steph drooling over his jade pieces and mooning about old masters' art works. He shipped a few items to the girl, who, unused to gifts (her Jewish father allowed her only $6 weekly allowance) was smitten by the treasures.

One afternoon Frank conveniently, fortuitously, finds Stephanie at home alone—ostensibly awaiting Aileen's return. She wearing the jade items he had sent (carried in her "muff"). Her presence seals the deal: Frank soon giving her more than jewels.

Stephanie conceiving of old Frank as a sort of artist in his realm, rather than simply businessman. What his art consisted of, besides genius for making money, was anyone's guess.

Cowperwood soon took over the West side railway. He was like an unstoppable force of the financial sector. In the love-sector however, he had a deuce of a time with Stephanie. Looking at her was like looking in a mirror for Frank. She too a "varietist"—a free-love sprite, involved with half-a-dozen others, but in manner unspecified. Frank turned suspicious with jealousy, wanting her to remain "true"; she said she was true (in her fashion). How the table had turned! Frank was not a happy camper. The taste of his own medicine choked him. He hired an associate to spy on Steph. The associate and Frank caught her in flagrante with another—Frank dropping her afterward like a hot potato.

Others were soon picked-up: all young things—daughters of his business associates (or wives). What could the snips of girls bring intellectually, emotionally, to the rendezvous? None were in the same ballpark as Aileen, emotionally; Aileen, 40-year old wife, now victim of a serial-seducer whose conquests clearly fed an insatiable need of glorifying a sickened ego.

Next in line for Frank a Mrs. Hand, young social-climber married to an old rich fogey. She gave handyman Frank, a hand or two; meanwhile, Aileen had been busy also, establishing a relation with one Polk Lynde (!), met in Bohemian circles he frequented. A kind of Beau Brummell and idle heir to a fortune.

The coming political contest promised to be fierce. Chicago was a democratic stronghold but ward-bosses had been known to change stripes attractive enough the quid pro quo. Cowperwood and his man McKenty, ex-officio boss man of the city, geared up against all the elements gathered, like politically potent Mr. Hand—outraged husband of the handy missus; old gas-men defeated in previously contested gas-wars; moralists determined to punish Frank for his improprieties; Schryhart, burned by Frank on street car and other dealings; and anti-Cowperwood newspapers (all five city dailies). A formidable array.

Cowperwood and his factotum were cooked in the election, a Republican victory. His enemies quickly moving to shut Frank out—end his dominance of the street car lines and his political entrenchment. Frank needing to fight for his political life in the scowling face of a new administration. A heavyweight like Frank pulled no punches however; he got some compromising goods on the new Mayor. An appeal to Democratic lieutenants, whose turn-coat behavior allowed the Republican victory, did not fall on deaf ears (some of those bosses feeling slighted by the spoils Republican victors offered).

Frank not idle on the woman-front either—or rather, the girl-front; a 15-year old privileged daughter of a Kentucky madam in his sights.

Berenice Fleming by name, a maiden of steel reserve—an inwardly seething type—kind of an Aileen—a "Circe(s) daughter." Berenice, Dreiser informed, appealed to old Frankenstein "as no other woman before had ever done."

Frank comparing the girl to Stephanie (recall Stephanie? The free-love chick who turned table on Frank?), only shrewder than Steph, and less evasive…In a rare moment of self-analysis frank wondered why he, a 52-year old man, would be attracted to a 15-year old girl? (The analysis ONLY momentary.)

When the nascent university of Chicago come calling, Frank dipped into pocket and gave, in an philanthropic instant, money enough to purchase a telescope and build an astronomy department.

Meanwhile, Cowperwood was having the dickens to secure funding to build a new elevated road, as the bankers were loath to loan, and the Mayor had pledged to forestall the project. What the Mayor did not yet know was that Frank had incriminating evidence of the moralistic Mayor's extra-marital proclivities. Old Frank was proving more adept a blackmailer than his enemies.

Aileen—remember her? Back at the ranch, and tired of her fling with Polk, the society playboy, took to the sauce—strong drink. Like any other nice guy, Frank cautioned her about excessive alcohol intake. Her scathing response to his caution worthy of any developing alcoholic.

Frank's enemies gave the old college try to squeeze him but he too wily to handle, and through machinations too complex to be adumbrated here, succeeded in making a killing when "American Match Company" went belly-up. Cowperwood crushing the opposition once again. If he were an ancient Roman surely he would have been assassinated. He put his newly earned moola into the building of a new home in New York City.

Fair Berenice had gone to the best girl's finishing school but her mother, Mrs. Carter, aka Hattie Starr, was reduced to near penury, thus becoming, of necessity, a madam. Berenice, unknowing of the mother's circumstances, was suddenly made aware—shocking knowledge altering her view of things. Her mother—poor! A madam! Knowledge also, that Cowperwood was paying the bills for the family's continuance.

Meanwhile Frank's Chicago career took a precipitate downswing with the gubernatorial veto of Frank-sponsored commission bill. For once, and perhaps only time, Frank's money did not buy his way to a proffered end. An idealist, and idealism, in this case, trumped materialism.

Berenice and mama were placed into a townhouse Frank purchased in NYC. Aileen, now living in the NY home, discovering the hidden life of Berenice and madam, confronted Frank, and proving, again, "there is no scorn like a woman scorned." The confrontation the most emotionally effective scene of the over-long book. Though why Aileen beat the old rug again is questionable. Most likely because she infected by the Cowperwood disease and would not take the antidote, which was to leave. Frank declaring he had lost love for her. She refusing to believe it. Her denial tragic, Homeric even. Cowperwood's emotional reach, compared to that of Aileen, puny and ignoble. Aileen went off the rails with thought of Frank's "adamantine character of soul." She throwing herself at him in one last gasp: and humiliatingly defeated. Her histrionics saddened Frank—while sad and wondering about the sadness of life, Aileen went upstairs and cut her wrist.

Deciding, after a spell, to follow her upstairs, he found the door to her room locked. After breaking down the door he found her in a bloody pool but still alive.

Dreiser turned his story into a stage play at ending. Played out in the chambers of Chicago's city hall where aldermen sat to vote on Frank's request for a 50-year lease on his street car lines, plus consolidation of the system. The aldermanic cabal surrounded by hoi polloi of the gallery— a mobocracy driven to fury by newspapers vehemently opposed and incensed by Cowperwood's reign of terror.

Frank spent a mill and a half bribery money on the politicians, but the money not enough. The people risen in moral fervor sent Frank down to defeat.

A dark day for our Frank—perhaps the end of his Chicago sojourn—but with one light in the darkness: Berenice, who had kept distance from her family's deliverer, suddenly yielding to Frank's power exuded from, Dreiser wrote, his "fascinating individuality."

Somewhat Carrie Meeber-like, Frank's restless heart continued to "hunger and thirst and wonder." The old urgent need for life, more life—and wealth, more wealth—like a lodestar forever in his vision.

THE GENIUS OF DREISER

Kirah Markham discovered Dreiser still in act and communion with Jug and left him. Despite separation in 1910 Theo and Jug continued hooking-up, intermittently, in the following 4-years.

Dreiser remained in his Greenwich Village apartment 5-yeas.

THE TITAN sold less copies than THE FINANCIER. Dreiser reportedly gaining no royalties from the publication so in debt was he to publisher's advances and loans. Living in the unconventional atmosphere of the Village in early 20th century America Dreiser felt comfortable enough to indulge his anarchistic steak—a facet of character colliding with the nonconformist though conventional prejudices of H. L. Mencken, and their affinity of relationship diminishing. (H. L. calling left wing writers "red ink boys").

Though supporting the war against Philistinism Dreiser retained his yearning for conventional success and wealth—a yearning for more, that ultimately made his life "an American tragedy of self-destructive ambition and abusive sexuality" (pg. 58, Lutz, Tom, AMERICAN NEVOUSNESS, 1903). "Driven by uncontrolled desire to make it big and feeling that he never really succeeded, (Dreiser) suffered from loneliness…until the end of his life" (pg.58, Lutz).

The war years of 1915-1919 activated Dreiser and Mencken to team-up, their mutual Anglophobia ("the despicable English aristocracy" Dreiser wrote) and Germanophilia uniting Herr Dreiser and Feldmarschall Mencken to "enthusiastic HOCHS" (pg. 183, Swanberg) over initial German victories. Each had to pipe the tone down with American entry into the war, in 1917—after a wave of xenophobia flooded the country. Sympathy for Germany verboten. Pro-German remarks brought jail-time for many. German Americans (Dreiser,

Mencken) became the new persecuted group: many of them, at this time, Anglicizing their names and putting a clamp on mentioning of heritage in the old country. The Espionage Act and Sedition Act legalized, encouraging the persecution.

Mencken's pre-publication review of Dreiser's novel THE GENIUS—completed by Dreiser in 1911 and revised 1913-14, begun the final freeze of long association between the pair. Mencken thought the novel "rambling, formless, chaotic." Mencken had an even stronger critical reaction to Dreiser's play "The Hand of the Potter." Both critical stances wrong-headed thought Dreiser, who felt that sex-perversion (as reiterated in his play) was simply another part of life, and as loathsome and revolting as the subject, still fit topic to write about—as any other aspect of life. Mencken feeling such topics should not be written about, but more or less swept under the rug in consideration of decorum and "common sense"—which he accused Dreiser of lacking.

Mencken had a non-conformist attitude but something of a conventional outlook. As Dreiser slid further to the left politically the friendship between the two slowly slid away.

NO GENIUS BUT TOM CAT

After THE GENIUS was published in 1915 Puritans tried stomping the work to death. The book's picture of a rake's immoral or amoral progress through life was unendurable for the censoring brigade. Before the book became too hot a property to tolerate, and was banned as blasphemous and obscene by the New York Society for the Suppression of Vice (pg. 203, Swanberg), citing 17 profane and 25-lewd passages, it had sold 8,000 copies, almost out of the gate—prepublication rep as a sex-fest translated into dollars. Dreiser's publisher John Lane pulled all copies from the shelves, thereby ending sales.

Though Dreiser instituted suit and sought help of the Author's League of America, the ban remained in place. 500-members of the League signed on to protest the ban (but not Hamlin Garland or William Dean Howells—pg. 262, Loving). The fight against the book's censorship led by H. L. Mencken, who, ironically, had disliked he novel, but believing the fight against the Comstock's a necessity, campaigned against the ban—which remained in place. (Not until 1923 and reissue of the novel, by Liveright, did sales begin again, the novel selling 12,000 copies within a year of publication and 48,000 copies in the next decade, earning Dreiser $25,000 (pg. 307, Loving)).

THE GENIUS

A small town in the American heartland—population 10,000. End of the 19th century. A town with 2-railroads and stations, 4-newspapers, and houses built of wood. John and Marian Witla lived there: with a son, Eugene, a good-looking lad, black-haired, even white teeth, almond-shaped eyes—but semi-anemic and overly sensitive; and a daughter, Myrtle. The father owned a sewing machine business, selling and repairing. A middle-class set-up.

Eugene but a fair student in school who cared nothing for grammar or mathematics (like young Dreiser). Did a little drawing and sometimes wrote, but mostly dreamt, either about girls or else of leaving the little town for an "elsewhere."

The father procured employment for the son, as typesetter and cub-reporter for a local newspaper. Along with the job Eugene simultaneously acquiring a girlfriend: blonde-haired conventionally-minded Stella Appleton, whom Eugene got to first-base with but no further (Stella not "that kind" of gal).

Experiencing fits of moodiness along with dissatisfaction, Eugene packed a bag and moved to Chicago, Illinois, 100-miles distant.

Chicago! Paved streets, gas lamps; the beat of hammers, ring of trowels; telegraph poles, factories, smoke stacks, church steeples; 10, 20, 30 railroad tracks side-by-side—shabby cars ("like beads on a string"). Moving trains, and people; dregs of beer, trucks of coal, brick, stone, sand…Chicago! "Like a great orchestra in the tumult of noble strophes," Dreiser wrote in NEWSPAPER DAYS.

Eugene securing a room for 2-dollars a week: wandering the streets, gawking like a hayseed. His nine dollars quickly running out. A job in a stove shop lasting only one day—quitting because bullied by another worker. Another job—as house-runner for a real estate agency. When the agency closed, Eugene signed on as driver of a laundry truck—a job Dreiser held as young man; so too Clyde Griffths, when on the lam in TRAGEDY.

On his route, Eugene met a working-girl in a laundry who introduced him to sex. Afterward, he felt like a "conqueror," Dreiser wrote, and that conquering or "owning" a woman gave a man an air of superiority and self-sufficiency (while non-conquerors or the seldom-conquering lacked the same?).

Hoping to increase his income Eugene went to work as debt-collection for a furniture company, another job Dreiser held in his young manhood.

In spare time Eugene drew pen and ink sketches. His sister once saying his sketches were good. He decided to enroll in a class at the Art Institute. After joining a nude-modeling class, he became familiar with one of the models, Ruby Kenning.

Returning home for a visit, after an absence of 2-years, Gene was introduced to Miss Angela Blue—who happened to live 75-miles outside Chicago. 5-years older than he, and more conventional in outlook and belief, the two becoming attached to one another despite differences. An odd case of "chemism."

Angela visited the city occasionally; Eugene visited Angela's home in Blackwood, Wisconsin. A large presentable conventional farm family. Angela sweet, pretty, but unavailable sexually. She saving herself for marriage. Eugene proposed to her though he not interested in founding a family but of a career in art. (Proposed even though also thought of marrying Ruby. A rogue of sorts, seemingly little conscious of anything outside of himself.)

A drawing instructor at the institute encouraged Eugene to seek work on a newspaper, and one of the poorer city papers hired him.

Eugene was not in love with Angela, but was in love with himself, it seemed; in love with being in love, perhaps—with himself as "lover" (a Romantic, with the Henry Miller virus).

He met with concert pianist Christiana and with Mariam Finch, likewise an artist. (They come in pairs: Angela/Ruby; Christiana/Miriam.)

Eugene the smart: reading Herbert Spencer, Marcus Aurelius, Schopenhauer…He lost his childhood faith—no more Heaven, or Hell. He read British thinkers: Darwin, Huxley, and wondered if life nothing but dark forces moved aimlessly?

Christiana gave herself to Eugene but had no interest in furthering the relationship—uninterested in marriage. Eugene was baffled, hurt; should not he be deciding the course of the relationship?

During the tryst with Christiana Eugene had ignored Angela—waiting back in Wisconsin. Memory of her fading in his mind. Norma Whitmore showed-up—another brainy-chick Eugene attempted to parlay with. She, Christiana, Mariam, all have it over Angela in the brain-department and art appreciation, but "Angel-Face" had her points—plus the marriage proposal still in the air.

Gene traveled to Wisconsin where he and Angela bound each other further with physical communion. The die cast: Angela had thrown herself onto his mercy and he binding himself in chains of duty and responsibility, neither of which he wanted.

Angela told Eugene: "if you don't marry me I'll have to kill myself."

Eugene looked at the water of the lake, imagining Angela in the water; he decided he would marry her; decided he had to marry her.

The couple moved into a studio-apartment in the Washington Square area of NYC. Weeks later, his passion dimmed, Eugene thought he had made a mistake—"put his head into a noose."

Eugene's city friends did not know what to make of the little wife-y. Miriam insulted Angela to her face; Norma froze her out; Eugene, oblivious to all but himself, had not heard the insult or recognized the freeze.

Gene's art work impressed a big art dealer come to the studio for a look. Gene of the Ash Can School of American art—Sloan, Bellows, Luks, Glackens, Henri, and others—realistic work of gritty often homely quotidian city scenes rendered dramatic through light and contrast.

The dealer showed a bunch of Witla's paintings in a downtown gallery, 3-pieces selling for $1300—enough money to stake Witla and wife to a season in London and Paris.

In Paris Eugene commenced where he left off in NYC. His a name now in the art world. Selling more work but becoming suddenly and mysteriously ill. Unspecified mental sickness he blamed on overindulgence in the bedroom—neurasthenia brought on by too much sex! Angela a kind of dynamo of lust after her long virginal years on the farm (she thirty to Eugene's twenty-five).

Eugene consulted a doctor of astrology—like Dreiser, always on the lookout for hunchbacks, horse shoes, cross-eyed men…The savant predicted 4-years of bad luck, and four of good.

Eugene and Angela returned to the states. The lad still not himself however—old stomach problems of youth returning. He could not muster effort to work. Down in the dumps, gloomy, under the weather. Angela not too spry either; she found letters from Christiana and Ruby sent to Eugene while she waiting for him on the farm. Eugene she realized had abused her trust.

A visit to the folks in Eugene's hometown occurring. A young lovely, Frida by name; another Stella Appleton—caught Eugene's roving eye. Angela, despite knowledge of his fickleness thought nothing of the flirtation.

Girlhood was Eugene's drug of choice. A comely 18-year old maiden the summum bonum of female beauty and attractiveness.

Angela come to; a confrontation occurring. Eugene deciding he hated his wife. "He cursed the day he had married."

The couple departed for Angela's home and family. At the Blue's ranch our man is blue, missing his "Frida." Angela Blue standing at his side—nauseating him. The blues moving him to leaving for Chicago. But Chicago not the inspiration he sought, so—elsewhere: here and there; his money dwindling.

An inability to work making him sicker—bringing on a morbid preoccupation with self—as Dreiser experienced following SISTER CARRIE's ill-treatment.

Eugene back in NYC, nearly broke. Angela returning to Wisconsin to stay with her folks.

Needing a job, Eugene pulled a Dreiser-move, applying to the President of a railroad—to a man known for his empathetic treatment toward artists down on their luck.

The President sent Eugene to work in a carpenter's shop as laborer. He boarded in the house of a friendly widow-lady. The widow's daughter Carlotta come to visit. A 32-year old woman—not really Witla's style, but—he lonely, plus little action since Frida back in the hometown (and no Angela). Inevitably the two come to understanding: she also married—and to a professional gambler.

Geno's illness due to a deprivation of life—which to him meaning love, of if not love, love-making.

The older widow caught wind of the affair between boarder and daughter. Emotionally fraught mother-daughter scenes enlivened the novel.

So self-centered a hero our Gene-O actually believing the women he had involved himself with had all benefited from the association; had gained in self-confidence—"had a better opinion of themselves for having known him."

Right.

Such oblivious self-serving arrogance! Self-aggrandized rationalization for predatory conduct. He had the "spiritual right" he believed, to play with the emotions of others. A free-love apostle: Witla as unnatural child of John Humphrey Noyes.

Angela, returning, fretted over Eugene's quondam loneliness and tribulations. Arriving like an angel of mercy and setting about saving him. Her gluttony for punishment insatiable.

Discovering Gene's ongoing affair with Carlotta sent Angela into a martyrdom phase which she must have enjoyed somehow, so often had she undertaken the role. Her wrath however, something to behold: equal to an Aileen Cowperwood-melt down. Witla, as Cowperwood, become ignoble-seeming worm in the storminess of such righteous agony and anger as Angela summoned.

Genie switching jobs—assigned to a mason crew run by a foreman named Deegan (called "Rourke" in Dreiser's great sketch "The Mighty Rourke," in TWELVE MEN). A fierce but fair-minded and compassionate pusher of men—a power onto himself.

Feeling restored, health-wise, Eugene went to work for a small newspaper as artist. From the paper he went to a big advertising agency as Art Director. He and Angela moved to an apartment overlooking West Central Park in NYC. Gene's $5,000 a year helped his outlook on life but the vicious and brutal job environment—put-out or get-out—hard to take. The high pressured corporate business world. He could not take it: resigned to take a less-demanding job—less lethal snake pit— as Art Director elsewhere. Salary rising to $12,000 yearly.

Climbing the ladder, he jumped to Advertising Manager for United Magazine Company, and even higher salary. The Witla's secured an apartment on Riverside Drive.

Through the wealthy publisher-boss of the outfit Eugene come in contact with delightfully gracious and alluring Mrs. Dale and her ravishing 18-year old daughter Suzanne. Witla licked his chops over such a prime cut of beef.

Gene swimming in gravy: the corporation he worked for making money hand over fist. When a certain Hebrew-looking fellow offered to set Gene up in a "can't miss" real estate deal Gene sunk his savings, 50K, into the proposed construction of a sea shore resort.

Witla slowly whittled his way to the enchantress, Suzanne—in Frank Cowperwood fashion—through proximity. 38-year old Mrs. Dale, supposed smart as well as beautiful, viewed the flirtation, Angela-like, without alarm.

So saccharine a pursuit! Not even Cowperwood stooped to such language: "Oh, Flower Face!" Eugene said. "Oh, Silver Feet! Oh, Mrytle Bloom!" It was a wonder the girl did not contract sugar diabetes. Witla had supped Love Potion #9—declared to the overawed girl that her presence brought him back to art again. Remember art? Witla painted once—he not only poet and businessman.

Angela discovered the affair, even if the mother had not. A dramatic scene occurring between her, Eugene, and Suzanne. Eugene shoved back against Angel Face, revolted by her tricks, her wiles (like the latest: she pregnant!). Suzanne, poor dear, little suspecting life to come with Witla: six months, a year, of lovey-dovey before being cast aside in favor of a new Juliet, or, if marriage, morphing into another drunken fish-wife like Aileen Cowperwood, or unhappy harpy like Angela becoming.

Suzanne deciding she would live with Eugene in a studio as soon as he left the wife. The wife's pregnancy however (a dirty trick!) muddled things; but still, Eugene planned a future with Suzanne—his life with Angela at an end, he vowed.

Suzanne let her mother in on the adventure. The mother went ballistic. A tremendous struggle of wills ensued. When reason and threats by the mother failed to alter Suzanne's planned life with Eugene, the mother tricked her daughter onto a train and whisked her away to a lodge in distant woods.

Gut-wrenching pages relating the mother-daughter struggle. Dreiser in his element yanking on heart-strings, until emotions become all but unbearable.

Eugene, despairing of his planned life with Suzanne, hatched a mad plan (like Hurstwood's capture of Carrie) of rescuing the girl from captivity.

Arriving at the lodge, Gene confronted the mother who gave him an earful, including pleas for more time in which her daughter might further consider her future—a plea Eugene considered—baffling Suzanne, who wondered why he did not whisk her away immediately—back to NYC and the planned life…But Gene not the heroic type as such—too diffident, cerebral perhaps, civilized; worried of threats the mother issued, such as exposing him by approaching his boss at United Magazine…Which she did, even though Eugene agreed to a waiting-period (before he and Suzanne riding off into the sunset together).

Resulting from his exposure as a scheming Lothario and stalker, Gene's boss—well known to Mrs. Dale socially—fired Eugene.

The loss of his 25K salary stunned Eugene; so did the freezing of his 50K sunk in the Sea Shore resort, which had floundered due to a lack of investment.

To top things off for Gene, Suzanne, threatened with loss of her inheritance, and a trip to an asylum, agreed to wait a year before joining him in a love-nest deal.

Under influence of his sister Myrtle, Eugene begun considering Christian Science and its peculiar mode of thought—a long disquisition on the subject interrupting the narrative (Dreiser's wife Jug turned to Christian Science in late adulthood).

Everything determined by Mind of God. Divine Mind. Evil as illusion. Humankind but a thought in the Mind of God.

Meanwhile, at the hospital, Angela suffered as imminent birth of her baby approached. A recently endured bout of rheumatism had weakened her heart—the condition alarming doctors—as did her age, forty-four.

A Caesarian section was unavoidable. The child was born healthy, but Angela died post-birth.

In the concluding chapter Dreiser used the "I" of authorial voice throwing off the consul of Marcus Aurelius, Spinoza, Schopenhauer, and Mary Baker Eddy, but leaving last words for Herbert Spenser in this wordy meticulously-wrought and ultimately beautiful novel.

POST NOTE

Perhaps the most perceptive review of THE GENIUS—among some awful and personally vindictive reviews—was written by John Cowper Powys, the English mystic and literary critic, who compared and contrasted the novel with Walt Whitman's LEAVES OF GRASS. Also noting Dreiser's "religious sentiment" while extoling the broad view of American culture contained within the novel.

ON THE ROAD

In 1916 Dreiser decided to accompany Franklin Booth, illustrator and artist—and fellow Hoosier, on a road trip, New York City to Indiana. Booth likewise lived in Greenwich Village and Dreiser had known him from his, Dreiser's, days editing magazines. Booth's car a 60-horse power Pathfinder, produced in Indianapolis and capable of speeds up to 45 mph. An 'open' car with detachable roof. A chauffer called "Speed," otherwise unnamed, driving and doing the maintenance work on the vehicle.

John Lane and Company provided Dreiser with $200 advance for a travel book.

A HOOSIER HOLIDAY

Not exactly Sal Paradise and Dean Moriarty on the road, but a daring trip, back in the day; without interstate highways or GPS. Driving on dirt roads much of the time.

After detouring in Pennsylvania to Binghamton N. Y., the adventurer's headed west into Ohio (Toledo, Grand Rapids) and southwest into Indiana and a tour of Dreiser's childhood homes, in Warsaw, Evansville, Vincennes, Terre Hault, and Sullivan.

Speed not only chauffer but something of a raconteur with stories of country people. Funny anecdotes Dreiser recorded. HOLIDAY is Dreiser's lightest in tone and most winsome book.

Dreiser foretold the demise of railroads in proliferation of automobiles; also, foresaw an American road system "unrivaled"—which did come to being.

He penned a little poem on the American flag: "the lifting aloft of the total stripes—red for blood and white for spirit and blue for dreams of man."

At a great transom bridge in Nicholsen, PA., Dreiser paused to indulge in what Richard Lingemen called "Dreiserian cosmic moodiness"—ruminating on fate and humankind's place in the universe.

Owego, N. Y., was "one of the prettiest cities we had yet found." Though pretty, "churches flourish, and theologically schooled numbskulls thrive," Dreiser wrote, while delivering an encomium on small town American life, praising its youth for vitality and the "force and zest" of its people—which not found in European towns he maintained—which he had visited. A theme that runs through A TRAVELER AT FORTY: the vital, yet gauche Americans—crude and untutored perhaps, but of an easy familiarity and lack of pretension.

On to Elmira, Corning, Bath, Portageville, Warsaw, East Aurora…

Life a romance to Dreiser, taking delight in a river or play of shadow in a glen—seeing beauty within the commonplace or even the ugly, like silhouette of a slag or coal heap against twilight sky. Noting scenes that "weave and sing."

Buffalo, N. Y., "crude manufacturing town," putting Dreiser in mind of past days as a young reporter unsuccessfully seeking work in the city. A time of American history called The Gilded Age, which Dreiser indicts as beginning years of injustices and inequalities within the country. Time of the development of great trusts, grown and become enthroned in the democracy, and seizing national privileges, bedeviling the law, poisoning the food, suborning the newspapers, and killing dreams of the folk. Time of the Robber Barons—multimillionaires threatening the life of the Republic: Rockefeller, Vanderbilt, Gould, Frick, Carnegie, Hanna, Morgan…The time of Grover Cleveland, Chester A. Arthur, Garfield, Hayes, and McKinley, 1870-1900.

Franklin and Theodore, the adventurous pair, entered a restaurant and were repelled by the joint's pretension and assumption of perfection—"a sort of raw uncouthness shining behind curtains of velvet. Vulgar gaucheries," Dreiser remarked.

Dreiser's tone of voice, generally mild, sometimes hectoring, particularly when considering religion, particularly Catholicism and its "priestcraft and ministerial conniving." In chapter 23 he went on a jeremiad against false prophets and would-be messiahs and the injustices committed by the Christian Church through the centuries. The tone leaking into other areas as well, such as manufacturing towns, like Buffalo and Cleveland, for example, where he detected a "spiritless drudgery" in workaday air—and leaking into inquisition—what read as such anyway, over the inequality of wealth between plutocrats and working-poor…

Outside Erie, PA., the trio drove onto marshy roads due to recent flooding—that had killed 35-people. They were shooed away by a cop on horseback. Dreiser told the cop "go to hell."

On to Ohio, the Buckeye state—so named for multitude of buckeye trees. In Astabula Franklin was hit-up by a ruffian for 15-cents. "Why 15-cents?" "To get rid of him."

Dreiser watched the "raw awkward and inept land pass" and was touched by a sense of youth and beauty and freedom and strength exhibited by the land's people, put forth in a vigorous, but "admittedly garish, way."

While thinking of picture postcards, which our narrator collected, he recalled the first he had seen, in Indiana as a boy. A memory leading him to other "firsts"—like first telephone, first bicycle, first roller-skate, first ice cream soda—a nostalgia trip.

At a Sandusky, Ohio, hotel, believing he was overcharged, Dreiser offered to fight the clerk, or, at the least, see the manager—but neither happened. Franklin, who had no stomach for confrontation, paid-up. On way to Clyde, Ohio, Dreiser fantasized beating the hotel clerk to death (killing the manager also).

Looking out the window, the old Roman (45-years old) grown ecstatic as the state of Indiana approached along the Maumee River. The air suddenly feeling different, he claimed; sky and trees and streets somehow sweeter. Feeling like he a "kid" again!

Mood-swinging.

Out of the industrial and manufacturing east and into the agricultural mid-west. Into scenery "so beautiful it was like a dream."

Approaching one of his boyhood homes—Warsaw, Indiana—his enthusiasm waned, and disappointment set-in over the fact, as he viewed the facts, "nothing had happened, and worse, nothing could." Over 50-

miles of road he had gone from near-ecstasy to depression over the lapse of time—30-years and all that had gone with it—friends, pleasures, aspirations...

South: into central Indiana; Wabash, Peru, Kokomo, Carmel. Dreiser recovering from the funk induced by childhood recalled in Warsaw, a time for him of deprivation. The more southern air seemed new to him, again; lighter, and the soil more grateful—"something romantic abroad," he claimed.

Doctor Dreiser, in a theological-non-denominational vein: Life! What was it? What made life life? It appeared incurably "varietistic" and pluralistic in tastes and emotions; appeared anachronistic...Undoubtedly a larger intelligence at work behind the scene—one that did not care for people but used humankind in some unknown fashion for purposes not understood. Call it, the user, "oversoul" (as Emerson did). The "power" or "product," perhaps, of something larger—a "God," as some said; a "Devil" as others said. "There is something back of man trying to do something, and Man is His medium, His bush, His paint. His idea." (pg. 28). God as artist-creator.

In any case, Dreiser advised keeping employed, suggesting employment the only surcease against the evil of too much thought.

Moving further south but with a new chauffeur, Bert, a crippled boy—in place of trusty Speed (fixer of multiple flat tires).

Indianapolis, Indiana, reminded Dreiser of Cleveland and Buffalo, also manufacturing towns, but Indianapolis without adjacent lake. All imitative of New York City and Chicago, he thought, and not of great interest...Onto Terre Hault, Dreiser's birthplace, where he spent his first seven years—"an unbroken stretch of privations and misery," he wrote. Thought of all the ills he endured rather than pleasures enjoyed. Outside of bad memories, the city OK: more vital-seeming somehow than, say, Sandusky or Fort Wayne (more like Wilkes-Barre, PA., and Binghamton, N.Y.). Further south brought our man to Sullivan, Indiana, where he experienced the same heartache as in previous stops at his childhood residencies over the evanescence of youth, of the past; though not as painful as in previously visited locales, as Sullivan where his imagination took over—hot and sultry land he later named "Egypt." A southern city where the mother and three youngest children maintained a house—Al, Theo, Claire. Fond memories of the romance of the railroad; the spectacle of trains moving twice daily into the switching yard taking or dropping off boxcars.

From Sullivan to Evansville where, Dreiser remarked, he begun to snap out his "dream period," coming to some understanding of reality, so-called. Another hot and drowsy southern city. Another two year stay for the Dreiser family. City where "darkies" and Germans abounded.

Thoughts of his brother Paul, who had rescued the family from poverty and moved them into a house in Evansville. A house owned by Paul's girlfriend, Sal, madam of an Evansville whorehouse.

After a hectoring screed on the dull unimaginative work of American architects, and the Philistines—those obtuse moralizers—Dreiser despaired momentarily over the state of the land, but—always there was breakfast to be had. Breakfast!

A feast of broiled squirrels. Only 60-cents a plate. Franklin wanted a mushmellon, but the waiter explained, "there ain't none to be had in the maaket."

"What? No mushmellons? Why the fields," Franklin exclaimed, "are full of them!"

"Da's right boss. Da's where they grows...But dey don't allus bring 'um down here. Dis ain't no maaket."

(A scene worthy of Melville—Stubb on deck the Pequod talking to the black cook.)

Memories of his brother were exchanged for those of his years attending Catholic Schools and churches, with black-garbed nuns, priests, other "ogreific" characters…A chamber of horror: corporeal punishment by whip and rod—the fear engendered! The difficulty of throwing off the oppressive weight of chains binding the communicant—the student.

At times Dreiser seemed solely contrarian but was, or could be, an optimistic sort believing in life's essential goodness, positivity—despite all else to the contrary—defeat, hate, death…A wondrous spectacle still, Life. With beauteous nature sylvan and delicate even—

On to Bloomington and visiting Theo's alma mater Indiana State University where he spent one memorable year, to him—as a "special student" (without customary high school diploma). One of the most "vitalizing" years of his life, he wrote. Arriving after leaving the work-a-day world of big city Chicago and plopping down in a verdant flower-strewn campus. What a contrast! From "pointless, unimportant bondslave to free, intellectual agent!"

Nostalgia bringing a burst of loneliness for our narrator. Gone the classmates, spread far and wide; none any longer in his orbit. "We are made to glow by the heat and radiance of certain days," Dreiser wrote, sighing over the faded and vanished life of the past.

Five states and 2000-miles. Was the trip worth it? Dreiser asked, but did not answer.

End of saga. Ended with hoping, wishing, for the Republic to continue, even though the great dream of democracy could not last, Dreiser thought—"cannot survive ultimately."

Franklin Booth's drawings accompanying the text a wonderful addition to the volume. Booth grown on an Indiana farm in Carmel, and learned to draw through a mail-order correspondence course. One day, taking some of his drawings to a local newspaper, he received payment for them. Booth was astonished, as was his father. Money to be made from art! Later, Booth attended the Art Institute of Chicago and the Art Students League in NYC. Of the dozen or so drawings produced in A

HOOSIER HOLIDAY my favorites were 'Terre Hault from West of the Wabash'—those clouds! 'Hicksville'—so fine the figures; as in 'Factoryville Bids Us Farewell'—the play of white light off of the store wall done to perfection! 'A Cathedral of Trees'—how fine those trees!

ENTER HORACE LIVERIGHT, 1917

Of Boni & Liveright. Publishers promising to republish all Dreiser's books and pay $500-$1000 advance on any new title.

Dreiser set-to working on volume 2 of his autobiography, NEWSPAPER DAYS. Also returned to short-story writing, publishing FREE, AND OTHER TALES with Liveright.

In FREE architect Rufus Haymaker yearned, longed—like so many Dreiser characters, for some ephemeral "it" (like Clyde Griffths, Carrie Meeber, Eugene Witla); more pleasure, beauty, meaning…Rufus is tortured, feeling trapped in a loveless marriage of convenience, and entertaining dark thoughts of his wife—lying in a sick-bed, near death. After she died, Rufus wondering if his ugly thoughts (wishing for her death) contributed to her demise. Perhaps precipitated her death?

In any case, her death, he felt, freed him. He was free! Free! But free to do what? Free ALSO to die!

"A parody of Dreiser's lesser novels," wrote Charles Shapiro (pg. 118, Shapiro).

How much of the story had to do with Dreiser's marriage? Feeling constricted by Jug—wishing he were with another (like Thelma Cudlipp). Jug refusing divorce. In 1914 she had signed an agreement to forego alimony, but in 1917 requested further financial support (pg. 277, Loving).

Boni & Liveright publication of FREE, AND OTHER STORIES included 11-stories written over a span of 20-years. The book sold 2200 copies in first few months post-publication (pg. 280, Loving) but critical reviews tepid.

The influence of Poe obvious to many Dreiser tales. "Convention," "Shadows, "Chains," and "Will You Walk Into My Parlor?" plunged readers into a paranoid and angst-filled world of narrator's slightly, seemingly, unhinged. Or are they? Suspicion and anxiety operative conditions characters endure or create.

Novella-sized "Will You Walk Into My Parlor?" competed with Dreiser's AN AMERICAN TRAGEDY is sustaining the pulse of suspicion and subliminal terror.

Ed Gregory, polished political operative of the story undergoes a trial by fire—all the ammunition of a despised political rival (corrupt Mayor of a corrupt city) used to discredit and incriminate Ed, in attempt to stop him from exposing the corruption. One of the Mayor's weapons—most powerful one—a beautiful young woman, Imogene (Imagine) who connived to spring a trap placing Ed in a compromising position (he happily married man).

So dastardly a plot! The ruthlessness of a Borgia; dialectical duplicity of a CP member. The other-worldly coldness of the young girl!

"Phantom Gold," one of Dreiser's comedic performances: an old farmer working a poor plot of land with aid of wife and two ungrateful selfish grown children was offered a substantial sum of moola by a prospector—after zinc discovered on the farmer's land. Trying to dupe his wife and children out of their shares of money the farmer received, sent the farmer into a mental tizzy; his chicanery and double-dealing nearly deranging his senses.

The idiom of the farm family's vernacular speech is queer and all but indecipherable in early stages of the story, but become quite comprehensible and fittingly apropos to the queerness of the characters and their constricted world, as the tale developed.

"The Old Neighborhood" another husband regrets-marriage story (see "The shadow," "Free," and "Married") featuring another brooder upon life's mysteries. Everything was alive, the narrator thought, "and everything was nothing, in so far as its seeming reality was concerned." A former rich-man on a nostalgic trip concerning his ex-wife; his present life mired in poverty—the whole trip like a self-inflicted wound.

"Saint Columba and the River."

Hydrophobic Dennis Glathery worked as a tunneler, of all things, and was nearly entombed beneath the river, while on the job. After his narrow escape from death he quit the job and begun praying to Saint Columba for succor (he is Catholic and of an Irish ferocity comparable to that of Rourke of Dreiser's sketch "The Mighty Rourke"). Economic factors drove Dennis back to the job, and he was nearly entombed again but saved when blown-out the tunnel and miraculously escaping death when continuing up through the earth and into and through the river. An escape through the Saint's intervention? Through dumb luck? Who could say for sure?

One of Dreiser's "best" stories," wrote Jerome Loving. "A story in which Dreiser contrasts a religious and mechanistic view of life" (pg. 258, Lehan).

"The Curse of the Idlewild" was based on a work-experience of Dreiser's. Another comedic performance, on par with "Phantom Gold." Quite different, the story, from the somber brooding Dreiser of "Hey Rub-A-Dub-Dub," a philosophical exercise (HEY RUB-A-DUB-DUB: A Book of the Mystery and Wonder and Terror of Life, 1920).

The purely ephemeral Idlewild story taking place in dry dock while a quondam "captain" and his "mate" (our narrator) run the quondam "ship" and "crew." Non-ship, non-crew, that is, as both were but railroad yard and workmen. Captain and mate have a fine time giving orders, while living their imaginary nautical life—as lived on the yachts in the river adjacent the yard.

Work could be boring. Playing make-believe lessened somewhat the dullness.

Most of the crew joined in the fun, participating in the extended ruse. A few did not—like the ill-disposed foreman, "lacking in imagination." A sourpuss, cement-face, without poetry in his soul (one in every barrel, or ship (yard)).

"The Mercy of God" stood as ruminative discourse on life's ultimate meaning and/or meaninglessness (similar to pondering aspect of HEY RUB-A-DUB-DUB). The story of the Homely Girl follows discourse. A girl lacking attractiveness the rest of the family possess: she devised a strategy for dealing with this fact. Strategy, or manner, or, to some—like her parents—"insanity." Consisting of her withdrawal in social situations by averting her face during encounters with men because she believes (explains, anyway) her appearance drove men wild.

Dreiser a similarly homely youth: front teeth protruding beyond his lips and "cast-eye" (right) (pg. 186, Loving). The feeling engendered by others' reaction to his image poignantly used in this story of survival.

TWELVE MEN

Published by Boni & Liveright in 1919, containing a series of essays, or sketches, considering 12-men of Dreiser's acquaintance. Including his brother Paul, father-in-law Mr. White, Muldoon of the Health Spa, socialist Mayor of Bridgeport, Conn., and others. Dreiser was better with a broad canvas to work on, but some of these sketches are wonderful. The book sold 2600 copies out of the gate and continued selling (pg. 180, Lingeman, vol 2.), and is still in print today.

LA LA LAND

Enter Helen Richardson, Theo's 2nd cousin. Age twenty-five, but looking younger (pg. 285, Loving), and claiming to be nineteen. Helen had, reportedly, a sex appeal that instantly attracted 48-year-old Dreiser. She had worked as secretary but was interested in acting and, at time she met Theo, 1919, was about to embark for Hollywood.

Dreiser joining her.

Tinseltown full of oil wells and movie studios (p. 288, Loving).

Despite her age, Helen was an old vaudevillian, having worked on stage as a child and working as part of a troupe, with her husband in West coast gigs, until she left him in 1918—to pursue other opportunities in New York.

While working as secretary Helen's boss gave her a copy of Dreiser's TWELVE MEN. She told the boss of her distant relationship to the great man and the boss urged her to contact him.

Initial optimism turned to boredom and distress for Dreiser in Hollywood ("City of the Folded Hands" he wrote). His screen plays rejected by the studios turned him to writing short stories and also working on another novel THE BULWARD, long in composition and already contracted for with a publisher. Meanwhile, Helen caught on at the studios and became sought after. She scored a role in "The Four Horsemen of the Apocalypse," staring Rudolf Valentino.

Dreiser had A BOOK ABOUT MYSELF—later titled NEWSPAPER DAYS, in the works as well. He also begun writing chapters of what would become AN AMERICAN TRAGEDY (first titled MIRAGE).

During his 2-year stay in California Dreiser wrote 24-chapters of the TRAGEDY (pg. 290, Loving), before returning to New York and Greenwich Village.

Dreiser continued his flirtations (and more) while living with Helen but her stepping-out on him, or even going-out, drove him into a rage. As upholder of the old double-standard, Dreiser's libertinism was and remained suspect.

Helen returned to the West coast for 7-months but bounced back to Dreiser. Her request that Dreiser divorce Jug went unfulfilled. As W. A. Swanberg noted, the last thing Dreiser probably wanted was marriage, as his estranged wife was a protection for his freedom (pg. 277, Swanberg).

TRAGIC AMERICA

Helen took an apartment in Brooklyn. Dreiser rented an office in the city where he wrote and did other things.

As Dreiser fended-off Helen's request of marriage he simultaneously carried on half a dozen other affairs, some of the women being employed as his typists and copy editors.

Work on his novel AN AMERICAN TRAGEDY had become the equivalent, he wrote Helen, to chipping stone off of a block. During composition he begun smoking cigarettes, despite his bronchitis; also resorting to snorts of gin for stimulation (pg. 236, Lingeman, vol. 2) or was it for deadening? Working as many as ten-hours a day on the manuscript—with assistance of at least two typists as well as editorial assistant (male) sent him by Liveright, Dreiser finished the book 11-25, after six years of thought and 2 and one half years of writing.

Based on an actual case—the 1906 murder of Grace Brown by Chester Gillette—Dreiser used, quoting from—sometimes verbatim—court transcript of Chester's trial. Dreiser had been looking for just such a case for many years: the man who murders his working-class girlfriend in order to marry a wealthier girl. "Interweavings of class and gender, of mobility and morality, and of ambition" (pg. 57, Lutz); money, class, desire, and dreams all conspiring to make AN AMERICAN TRAGEDY.

AN AMERICAN TRAGEDY

Clyde Griffths, protagonist, twelve years old as the story begun, living in Kansas City, in a mission—"The Door of Hope"—with evangelical parents, younger brother, and two sisters. Theirs a poor lot and Clyde, sensitive and materialistically-inclined, felt acutely the stigma and dreariness of his place in life.

Against his parent's wishes, Clyde determined he would go to work, and begun working in the basement of a 5 & Dime store. Shortly afterward, he begun working at the lavish position, to him, of assistant soda jerk in a shop next door to a movie theater. His education in the world had begun, offering knowledge of all kinds of people whom his parents would not have approved of.

Running an errand outside the soda shop one day, Clyde approached the boss of another shop, seeking to find himself more lucrative employment. No openings were to be had but the proprietor referred Clyde to the adjoining hotel where he met the captain of the hell hops and was hired.

Feeling and early cravings of Clyde's—his consciousness—presented an initial and immediate problem. For the sense, his sense, of his life being circumscribed and something shabby and little—how to believe Clyde capable of such distinctions, such judgements? All he had known in life, his life, in a variety of mission houses, were the circumscribed, shabby, and little. From what reference point did he decide on the unimportance of his father and the cheapness of his surroundings? He had read no books; he had no contact with anyone outside the rounds of missionary work—where did the capacity for reflection and subsequent judgement come from? When he went to work as bell hop at the Green-Davison Hotel he felt himself superior, knew himself to be better educated, than his peers, the other bell boys; yet, had received no other education either—not in a regular sense, so where did the discernment and education allowing him to make the value judgements, in which he discovered himself, and family, to be somehow lacking or less than? These judgement and discernments were not the ideas of Clyde at all, but those of Theodore Dreiser—as a youth. Which presents a difficulty in early sections of the novel, for there was a discrepancy between the blandness of Clyde's portraiture and his corresponding power of taste, judgement, and discernment. Where derived Clyde's standard of taste? The author assured the reader that Clyde is a most ordinary fellow—oversensitive perhaps, and dreamy, but otherwise a perfectly bland and homogenized youth. Which raises a dichotomy—between the perspicacious Clyde and ordinary Clyde—that threatened verisimilitude. Only a genius child such as Dreiser could have had the capacity of such distinction-making. Clyde no genius—not presented as such, yet his sagacity suggesting an extraordinary perceptiveness. That this questionable sagacity does not matter to the rest of the story—to Clyde's development as ambitious and facile individual—and near cipher without much capacity for reflection—is the triumph of the novel. Clyde's magical beginning years subsumed in quotidian life as bell boy, junior executive, and, finally, murderer.

The Green-Davison is the naïve boy's introduction to vice. In company of bell hop associates Clyde encountered all his religious parents had warned him against.

The bell boys took-up Clyde because, in part, they sensed a certain superiority of demeanor in him. He looked down on their guttural speech and coloration of vernacular yet envied their seeming lack of inhibition and worldliness.

The captain of the bell boys named "Squire." Clyde's immediate supervisor, "Mr. Whipple." The hours were six to noon, then six to midnight, every other day; the other 3-days, noon to six only. 66-hours weekly. Salary of $15 weekly plus board.

The other bell boys: Heggland, Ratterer, Kinsella, Doyle, Higby, and Shiel.

The oldest Griffths' girl, Esta, disappeared one day; believed to have run off with a masher.

The sum of money—at least $6 a shift in tips, seemed astronomical to Clyde. Geez!

On an off-night Clyde followed the boys to a bar and can-house. Though never having "known" a woman—or had a drink of alcohol, he did both that night, and felt no worse for wear either. At Ratterer's place Clyde met a "crude shop girl," pretty and dark Hortense Briggs, a "silly" who "no more knew her mind than a moth." (Knew what she wanted though.)

Clyde the greenhorn lost his mind over attractive Hortense. The pair seemed a good match: vain and shallow Clyde and self-obsessed Hortense; but Clyde a lamb to Hortense's lupanar. A rookie of romance against a pro.

Esta, the runaway sister, showed up back in the city after some months away, pregnant and abandoned. The mother asked Clyde for money for Esta but he loathe to give. Needed some fancy duds to keep up with Joneses in the sartorial department—plus Hortense is pumping him for jack like he was an oil well.

A friend of one of the bell boys offered to take the group—5 boys, 5 girls, out driving in a car he, the friend—Sparser—borrowed from his employer. The outing as planned but on return trip heavy traffic, snow, making the boys late and, fearful of losing their jobs, urging Sparser to more speed. He then running over a child in the city street and—thought of disgrace and trouble, having taken the car without owner's consent—running the vehicle, in a panic, onto a construction site and crashing.

Clyde, along with others not incapacitated, running from the law—thus begun his, Clyde's, life on the lam.

Book II. Lycurgus, N. Y., a city of 25,000 mid-way between Utica and Albany, New York.

The home of Samuel Griffths; he of the Griffths Shirt and Collar manufacturing concern.

Dinnertime in the imposing but not ostentatious house on Wykeagy Avenue where the Lycurgus wealthy reside. Samuel, Mrs. Griffths, Myra the oldest daughter, Bella the youngest, and Gilbert the only son and heir apparent.

The father broke news of Clyde, of the Western-branch of the Griffths family, coming east to work in the collar and shirt business. (Clyde's father, Asa, the estranged brother of Samuel.)

Samuel set-up Clyde and begun his downfall really, from the get-go, by instructing the family not to pay the boy attention—"not the slightest." A remark leading to Clyde's isolation, causing him much grief until his unhappy ending.

After the accident in K.C. Clyde had made his way, through subterfuge, to Peoria then Chicago and to a job working as a laundry truck driver (one of Dreiser's youthful jobs). Delivering to a club one day, Clyde run into his old bell boy chum from K. C., Ratterer. And Ratterer, in turn, advising Clyde how to get on as bell boy in the club, Union Club, a swank joint that politicians and wealthy businessmen—like Samuel Griffths—frequented.

On the qui vive for such opportunities, Clyde introduced himself to his Uncle, who agreed to give Clyde a chance at making good in the factory in Lycurgus.

Samuel one of three Griffths' brothers; Clyde's ineffectual father Asa, one; Allen, another; and Samuel. Allen and Samuel had shared their father's $30,000 inheritance while Asa, Clyde's father, left out of the will—a fact causing Samuel guilt—a factor in his hiring his nephew.

The Griffths factory six stories high, 1000-feet in length, employing over 800-workers.

Clyde walked into the office of his cousin Gilbert on his, Clyde's, first day of reporting for work. Gilbert ("Gil") was icily condescending (sight unseen, disliking Clyde—who had a marked resemblance to Gil).

Company executives Smillie, Latch, Gotboy, and Burky (Turnkey) welcomed Clyde into the fold.

Clyde assigned to a menial job in the "shrinking room," in the basement of the operation (salary $15 weekly). His direct supervisor a Mr. Kemere (Com'ere!).

Lodging at Mrs. Cuppy's "dull dubby" boarding house, Clyde made acquaintance of Walter Dillard, a socially ambitious working chap who begun dancing attendance upon Clyde—solely because Clyde a "Griffths"—a name with clout in Lycurgus.

Dillard set-up Clyde with a girl: Rita Dickerman. After a date with the eager and obliging Rita, Clyde is tempted to follow-up, seeking her favors, but an invitation from the Griffths—finally condescending to acknowledge their nephew's existence—arrived, inviting him to dinner.

During dinner at his Uncle's Clyde was introduced to a friend of the family's, Sondra Finchley, whose beauty took Clyde's breath away and whose savoir faire and charm caused Clyde to abandon, completely, thoughts of Rita Dickerman.

After 5-weeks of work Clyde was pulled out the basement and made a supervisor in the stitching department, where he had charge of dozens of women and girls.

Girls! Clyde could not help looking or starting to fantasize. Ruza, Martha, Flora; late summer afternoon air turning people languorous in the factory. A strictly enforced company policy forbidding fraternization between the help and supervisors existed, but, still: girls—girls—so sensual, appealing; hard keeping his mind on business for Clyde; hard to resist not drawing closer to some of them—but keeping always the warning of Gilbert on fraternization in mind; keeping, too, memories of Hortense Briggs in K.C.—the trouble that relationship caused him!

Enter Miss Alden, a lamb, from Trippet's Mills, 50-miles distant Lycurgus (though she originally from Biltz). A poor working-girl delightful of appearance. Daughter of honest, respectable, god-fearing farm folk. A pretty girl—god how pretty! Prettiest of all, to Clyde.

He fought against the protesting libido of his nature, and lost. Loneliness driving him as well—no friends since moving from Miss Cuppy's establishment (to avoid overtures of Dillard and other lower-placed companions in hierarchic Lycurgus).

A chance meeting—what else, in Dreiser's coincidentally-wrought and magically-infused fictive world? Bringing he and Roberta together, at Crum Lake, a canoe ride in the offering: she, before boarding: "is it safe?" Ha! A bit of foreshadowing, in dreadful fashion, of events to come.

Roberta—Miss Alden—left her rooming house room, at Clyde's urging, and her acquaintances, taking a private room in a private house. Clandestine meetings of she and Clyde proceeding. An "ecstatic paradise," Dreiser wrote, begun in the center "of a humdrum conventional and petty and underpaid work-a-day world."

One day Clyde, receiving an invite to a party at the Trumballs, met there the creme de la creme of youthful Lycurgus society, including the beautiful Sandra Finchey again—a "seeking Aprodite"—a "less savage, although scarcely less self-entered Hortense Briggs."

The invite to the party issued, unknown to the Griffths—not bothering with Clyde since his one home visit—a purposeful exclusion fed by Gilbert and his mother's snobbishness.

A 2nd invite following, again from the Trumballs (influenced by Sondra, thinking of Clyde as possible suitor; also thinking of embarrassing

Gilbert Griffths whom she heartily dislikes), bringing Clyde to a pre-Christmas party. His presence there despite his intention to share Christmas Eve with Roberta—begun a tearing away, like a layer of skin, from affection.

Instead of being honest with Roberta—as to his proclivities elsewhere (with the Trumballs, Finchleys, Starks, et al.) Clyde making alibies—lies. Beginning feelings of his pity for her risen—her unenviable position as 2nd best—to Sondra.

Clyde never saying he would marry Roberta. Certainly not, with fair Sondra, heir to the Finchley Electric Sweeper Company, in the wings.

Dissembling his emotions, Clyde insisting he does still love Roberta; in fact; regarding her first in his heart (not!). Said with Sondra fixed like a star in his affection and desire.

Clyde, finally summoning the courage making a break from Roberta possible, was told, by her, of her pregnancy. Clyde's "clear knowledge," as Dreiser wrote, of contraception, clearly not adequate.

Preggers! A game changer.

The news precipitating Clyde into a series of befuddled actions: pleading with a druggist for a remedy (and being sold a worthless $6 box of pills); talking with a haberdasher of his acquaintance—one Orin Short—as to the name of an out-of-town doctor—who come up short subsequently as to providing an operative remedy.

Roberta determining that Clyde should marry her.

A letter from Ratterer to Clyde, his bell hop friend, informing Clyde that 3-months the term during which anything, in amelioration of the condition, might be done.

Three months passed; the insoluble problem remaining. Roberta agreeing to return to her home and awaiting Clyde to come for her.

He reading a story in a newspaper about an accidental—or otherwise—double drowning on a nearby lake. And the finding of the woman of the presumably drowned couple, but not the man. Could have the man, surviving, run off?

Clyde thought of such an accident happening to Roberta. If so, he would be free. Free! Free to marry Sondra and enter the paradisiacal realm she and family represented to Clyde.

Meanwhile, Clyde becoming regular up at the Twelve Lakes colony of rich people, Finchleys, Trumballs, Wyants, Starks, et al. Oh if only—to belong—to enjoy—to have Sondra permanently in his arms!

He took note of isolated spots, lakes, of the region. Begun to plot, however unconsciously, Roberta's demise (that newspaper story!). He heard the wier-wier bird call from the forest one day; listened to an efrit, substance of some diabolic wish or wisdom—voice of his darkening self, another day.

Meanwhile, Roberta, still at her parent's home, growing frantic for Clyde to come for her; she penning a threatening note: "the world will know how you have treated me…My whole life is ruined and so will yours be…"

On a train, Roberta and Clyde. Taking a short honeymoon in the Lake region before being married.

Roberta and Clyde in a rowboat out on the surface of the water of isolated Big Bittern Lake. Floating in the bay—water like a black pearl. Clyde felt some embracing arm on him—like some demon steeling him to commit the deadly deed held in his mind.

Roberta sat in the stern; since entering the boat she seemed, to Clyde, to have faded, become insubstantial somehow—become illusion, more vaporous than real…

Roberta, in the water, crying for help (she could not swim). Clyde swimming away from her to a new life, or, so hoping.

Finding the boat floating in the water; trolling for bodies. A woodsman named John Pole fishing Roberta out the drink.

The county's District Attorney, Orville Mason (a Mason?) needing a doctor to perform an autopsy: Lincoln of Coldwater is suggested; Mason settling for Webster of Utica.

A search of Clyde's room in Lycugus: the finding of Roberta's letters sent (he had saved them!). The D. A. sending Sheriff Slack and his German contingent of deputies, Kraut, Sissel, and Swenk. Boating to Bear Lake, picking-up Clyde gamboling with his rich friends.

Inexorable law like a bulldozer moving forward. Dreiser the virtuoso, plucking heart stings for all he was worth (which was plenty).

The Griffths lawyer, Brookhart, sent to visit Clyde in the jailhouse; the lawyer sending another lawyer, Catchuman, to cross-examine. He giving way to two local lawyers, Belknap and Jephson.

The camera of Clyde's, inadvertently striking Roberta in the face as she leaned toward him in the boat, was trademarked "Sank."

Clyde declared "mental and moral coward" by his lawyering pair. Kidnap and Jetson. (Dreiser earlier told of Clyde's "feverish urgent disposition" not concerning itself with "more than the most immediate cares.")

Unstable and flighty Clyde. But "coward" too? His fear seemingly real enough: to be fired for fraternization and subsequent loss of income as well as standing; to lose his dream of marrying the rich girl…His lawyers mentioning his, Clyde's, "perhaps too pliable and sensual and impractical and dreamy mind." Perhaps?

Clyde's mother, in Denver, hearing of his conviction and moving like a tornado out the West to be at his side. Setting about raising money for an appeal.

Clyde, meanwhile, on death row, thinking about "the chair."

Richard Lingeman on the mother returned: "The Oedipal triangle is resolved, the mistress-mother lost, the wife-mother dead; the real mother reasserts her claim: "my son—my baby," she cries in her last PIETA embrace" (pg. 154, Lingeman, vol. 2).

Clyde taking consul of Nicholson, a lawyer, on death row for poisoning a rich old man. But Nicholson frying, leaving Clyde alone again—alone! His mother returned to Denver—to care for sick husband.

Alone and condemned to die. But he innocent! He did not mean to kill Roberta—though plotting to do so—inadvertently striking her; her falling, as he; the boat overturning, striking her on the head—an accident! But he hearing her cries and not going to her—that his sin, his crime, extenuating guilt...

Visiting Reverend McMillan revived Clyde's spirits, offering a spiritual solution to his problems. Clyde deciding to confide in the Reverend but how to explain the madness assailing him—at time of the...accident? The lunacy—he now realizing—seizing him in his pursuit of the wonderful Sondra. The desire driving him, literally, out his mind. Would a Reverend understand that desire? Any more than the twelve-man jury that convicted him?

The Reverend failing to fathom the depth of all-embracing desire. Mystified and troubled by Clyde's confession.

In an audience with the governor of the state, and Clyde's mother—a last minute plea for Clyde's life—the Reverend not denying he thought Clyde guilty as charged—thus ending possibilities of commutation of sentence.

Dreiser took one of his great fears, hydrophobia—or in his case, aquaphobia, and made of it subject of his novel. Hydrophobia being a symptom of contracting rabies. Barring Dreiser's contact with rabies, he suffered the anxiety disorder of aquaphobia—an irrational fear of water and/or drowning. His fear resulting, he wrote in A HOOSIER HOLIDAY, from a childhood episode whereby his brother Rome begun rocking a rowboat he and Theo were in on the river, outside their Sullivan,

Indiana, home. Though in DAWN Dreiser wrote of his being in the boat with Rome plus two other siblings, and the rocking made not by Rome but by the wake of a passing steam-propelled steamboat. (In DAWN Theo also related that he walked in his sleep as a youth—once walking out a 2nd story window! Certainly the action of an anxious disposition.)

NOT AS TRAGIC

Dreiser left New York with Helen to escape the bad reviews he expected, post-publication the TRAGEDY. Like Mencken's review, published in the American Mercury: "a vast, sloppy, chaotic thing of 385,000 words—at least 250,000 of them unnecessary."

Mencken's view a minority decision. Most reviews were positive, even laudatory, like that of James Wood Krutch, published in The Nation: "the greatest American novel of our generation" (pg. 312, Swanberg).

Within a month the TRAGEDY had sold 13,000 copies (pg. 26, Lingeman, vol. 2).Dreiser eventually raking in 47K in total royalties (pg. 280, Lingeman, vol. 2). He woke and found himself wealthy. In 1926 he and Helen vacationed in Europe for four months. After returning to the U. S. Helen found her "dream home"—a $3,000 monthly duplex across from Carnegie Hall.

Helen had become known as the woman Dreiser always returned to. "Dreiser was my religion," she had explained—like a good masochist (pg. 320, Swanberg). Dreiser came and went as he choose, often leaving Helen alone at night. At this time, the two slept in separate beds (pg. 284, Lingeman, vol. 2). Feeling lonely and abandoned, Helen conducted an affair with a Hungarian pianist. Dreiser, told of the affair—by Helen—had thrown a fit. Helen dropped the pianist.

In the fall of 1930 Sinclair Lewis (BABBIT, MAIN STREET, ELMER GANTRY) was awarded the Nobel Prize for Literature over fellow novelist Theodor Dreiser. One of the more myopic decisions ever made by the Stockholm crowd (Pearl Buck over Dreiser a few years later, even worse). It is possible, as Jerome Loving suggested, that the disappointed Dreiser, feeling his placement below Lewis in literary hierarchical terms, the reason he gave up writing fiction, until last years of his life.

Dreiser the anti-capitalist invested heavily in Wall Street stocks and bonds. He also spent heavily on a country home he had built on an estate at Mount Kisco, north of NYC. This summer home he called "Iroki," Japanese for "the spirit of beauty" (pg. 32, Pizer, Donald, Literary Masters, THEODORE DREISER, vol. 7).

In the fall of 1927 Dreiser had accepted an invitation to visit the Soviet Union. His stay in Russia lasted 77-days (pg. 337, Loving), and turned him into a de facto Communist and cheerleader for the CP though always, personally, as he stated, "an individualist." His individualism keeping the Party from accepting him into membership.

The trip also seemingly turned him toward social activism. He become a pamphleteer and reformer—work which took precedent over his fiction-writing which, until his posthumous publications, had ended.

In 1929 Dreiser published a book of sketches titled A GALLERY OF WOMEN, which did not do as well, sales wise, as his TWELVE MEN—because, Mencken wrote, "men are more interesting"—or maybe had more opportunities to be interesting? Critical reviews of the work favorable but unenthusiastic (pg. 327, Lingeman, vol. 2).

The stock market crash of October, 1929, wiped-out half of Dreiser's capital (pg. 353, Loving).

Iroki become reflection of Dreiser's confusion—his unstable changeable mind, holding contrary ideas simultaneously, switching plans and course mid-stream—leading to creation of an architectural jigsaw puzzle, with totem pole out front. Five different artist's-architect's consulting on the project (pg. 358, Swanberg). "A substitute for the infant (Helen) and Dreiser never had" (pg. 252, Lingeman, vol. 2).

In 1930 Dreiser again turned to the writing of DAWN, autobiography of his earliest years. He retired to Iroki to write, and with assistance, begun revision of a work he had begun as early as 1911.

Meanwhile, the firm of Horace Liveright, previously Boni & Liveright, went under due to the depression. Dreiser had weathered initial depression years, and a payment of $55,000 from Hollywood—for a talking version of AN AMERICAN TRAGEDY—unlike previous film made of the book— helped solvency.

Having stopped writing novels, Dreiser had thrown himself into so-called leftist action in defense of the Scottsboro Boys, Tom Mooney, and the United Mine Workers strike in Pennsylvania. He had become a go-to voice of protest for the left and the Communist Party.

DAWN incensed his sister Mame—living now at Iroki, along with Dreiser's brother, debilitated Rome, whom Theodore had killed-off in A HOOSIER HOLIDAY, then had discovered living in a Chicago care-home. Mame took care of Rome. DAWN appeared in print in 1931. Despite dealing with early years of Dreiser's life the book published after vol. 2 of the autobiography, NEWSPAPER DAYS, dealing with later years. DAWN was withheld from publication so as not to offend the family.

DAWN

What “soul”? A something; a spiritual whatever. Where from? Is such but energy—the physicist’s broken atom? Energy the fierce spirit of the universe (a mechanistic universe).

And humankind? Made from blood & energy of the parents or from an independent source? Who could say?

Dreiserian speculations of a boy growing up in the American Mid-West, last quarter of the 19th century. The dry mostly waterless plains of Indiana, the “Hoosier” state. No longer “Land of the Indians,” but “Hoosiers”; that is, backwoodsmen, country bred, country bumpkins…

A land “miasmatically puritanic” and “patriotic,” Dreiser wrote, and bred to ignorance by the world’s “greatest rostrum vendor”—the Catholic Church.

In Vincennes the dreamy impractical mom resided, with the three youngest children of the family, in a combo firehouse/whorehouse; until a move made north—a few hours as the crow flies, to Sullivan, and a new home by a slaughter-house. The mother took in laundry and boarders to make ends meet—though they never did. For Theo and his brother Ed, their two years in Sullivan were shoeless days.

In Sullivan Theo developed his Thoreauvian love of the natural world. Rising at four in the morning to go out walking, with his mongrel dog “Snap” to examine spider webs, morning glories, trumpet flower, bluebirds, swallows, wrens, house martens, larks, Gopher holes, wasp’s nests, crawfish, salamanders…To look and brood on the multifarious forms and mysteries of origins—the strangeness of the life: bats, bees, skunks, snakes, rabbits…the nature-idle interrupted one day when a farmer acres away took a pot shot at Theo’s dog!

Lonely hours, days, of childhood passing in solitary walks or playing games of his own devising, like "train," a game of moving boxcars in form of cigar boxes across the floor or across the yard, he conducting them hither in replication of the whistle heard from nearby freight yards.

After being picked-upon by two local bullies, Theo and Ed lived circumspectly—as to coming and going—until brother Al showed up, off the farm where he had been working, on a relative's spread up north, and routed the bullies—making his younger brother's lives more bearable.

From Terre Hault, north of Sullivan—where Dreiser Senior was working and living—with four of the Dreiser daughters—the girls, together or separately, begun arriving in Sullivan, fleeing the wrath of the father's patriarchal and religious-based, rule. The mother a lax overseer of the daughters, who ran about, innocently enough, but with destructive results.

A big day for Theo come when opening his first book, "Hill's Manual," a how-to volume (how to write a business letter; how to hold a fork while eating) bought, or traded for, by the mother off a boarder, a man known as "Professor."

Escape for the family from Sullivan come via the largess of long-absent eldest child Paul, arriving like the Santa Claus of yore (having the girth too). Distributing gifts and money and taking the family to a new home in Evansville, south on the Indiana-Kentucky border. The house owned not by Paul but by his mistress, Sallie Walker, madam of an Evansville house of ill repute.

Paul worked as star comedian at the Apollo Theater in Evansville and supplying money to the family though not telling his mother as to the profession of his inamorata.

When things were in disarray in the home-life the mother would threaten to leave—walk-out; an action changing the children's attitudes immediately.

After two years in Evansville, Sallie and Paul had a falling-out, and the Dreiser's needed, again, to move-on. Following three of the sisters, the family relocated the distance of the state, to Chicago, a city of over half-a-million residents, at the time.

Theo and his brother Ed becoming newsboys, hawking The News in the streets, at 1-cent per copy.

The great city! Panorama of ship traffic on the lake; call of the street vendors; parade of humankind in the byways: excitement! Glamour! Expense!

The family could not hack it, soon vacating the city for Warsaw, Indiana, in the state's northeast. Years in Warsaw coinciding with Theo's 13th to 16th years. A flowering period for him emotionally. Sent for the first time to Public School: a revelation for Theo—twenty-one and two year old female teachers. Soft-eyed and kind May Calvert, Theo's seventh grade teacher, cooing and affectionate. The positive attention he received meaning all the world to one so placed as our Theo. Girl students as well! Lovely as corn flowers, but Theo bashful and frightened of them, and had determined somehow he too homely, unqualified like other boys for affection.

Books coming into prominence in young Theo's life. The family knew him as bright, encouraged his reading, even the father: purchasing sets of Thackeray, Scott, and Dickens, for Theo's use. Theo dipping into each—a key as to where some of Dreiser's old fashioned-seeming language come from.

The end of the 3-year long Warsaw adventure come at the hands of broken Rome and the elder sisters whose actions brought the disrepute of class-conscious moralistic townsfolk. Rome the drifter returned to the family bosom and continuing drunken ways and lawless shenanigans and the girls fooling with local Beau Brummel's, entering into all sorts of illicit romances. Two of the girls returning to Chicago and marrying; another daughter impregnated by a local ne'er do well, and she being sent to live with another daughter to have the baby. The disrepute moving others to exclude Theo and family members as undesirables.

Theo lost his virginity to the baker's daughter: a near rape—by the girl, of Theo.

Theo also first experienced self-pleasure, aka self-abuse, wondering what had occurred and if it harmful? Turned to masturbation Q 3 days. Much worrying about the practice on his general health.

Meanwhile, one of the married daughters was deserted by her husband; the pregnant daughter sent her child back to the mother to raise; the father suffered bladder problems.

Things not all bad however: two of Theo's teachers took solicitous attitudes toward him, one counseling Theo to ignore the nasty things others said about his family; also telling him he had a good mind and bright future, despite his present worries.

Drawn to science and history but lacking the particular "chemical bias" for serious detailed technical endeavor, Theo gravitated to art and philosophy. Never a specialist, but capable of general theorizing.

No idea, he claimed, or only vague ones, about writing. After immersing himself in a study of Dickens, he turned to Thackeray until, as a young reporter in Pittsburgh, to Balzac.

The Superintendent of Schools recognizing Theo's advanced mental capabilities, encouraged the boy to further study. The Superintendent plus a few teachers gave Theo impetus to continue studying, when due to life circumstances he could easily have given up.

Battling a severe inferiority complex, Theo failed to grasp opportunities life afforded, thinking himself unworthy—despite praise received and recognizing the growing power of his mind. His bashfulness like an anchor attached to self.

At age sixteen Theo, deciding to leave Warsaw for Chicago, packed a bag and told his mother farewell. She gave him $6 and a box with a lunch inside.

Chicago, strong, rough, shabby. $1.50 a week room; Theo looked out his room window at yellow horse cars—maybe owned by Charles T. Yerkes (Frank A. Cowperwood).

He found a job as pearl diver in a Greek restaurant owned by John Papalopalopalopalopalous. He disliked the kitchen odors and accumulated filth of the place (pee-u! I been there).

Visiting his sister, she and Theo contrived a plan bringing the mother to Chicago and reuniting the family. Theo told his sister he was a clerk receiving $7 weekly—not a dishwasher making $5 weekly (pride!). His next job was in a hardware store cleaning stoves—a job young Eugene Witla worked-at. Like Witla, Theo lasted only a day or two—being driven off the job by a bullying employee.

Marcus Romanus, the wayward Dreiser, showed up in Chicago, getting Theo a job on the railroad which, like so many of his other jobs, did not pan-out.

Next for Theo another hardware warehouse concern. There he met another worker, Aaberg, a cultured but dissolute fellow, intellectual, who led Theo to thought that the mind alone “makes the essential difference between the classes and the masses.”

Dreiser’s “angel tendencies” of mooning about and day-dreaming nearly soon ended his career in the practical commercial warehouse venture. Discharged by one boss, he fell onto the shoulder of a more sympathetic boss who kept Theo employed for additional months.

The hardware store become history with the advent of Miss Fielding, Junior High School teacher, returning to Theo’s life. The saintly Miss offered her ex-student a paid year of study at Indiana State University.

Goodbye hardware store: hello groves of academia—in Bloomington, Indiana.

Theo not overly excited by college; not seeing the point of regurgitated knowledge; not feeling drawn to any one subject in which to specialize…As Aaberg the ill-placed wastrel savant of the hardware racket, so Sutcliffe, a Hindoo-like student-scholar of depth whom Theo claimed to have learned more from than the professors.

Also the girls. So many girls! He becoming intimate with one but having embarrassment and chagrin of premature ejaculation. Deepening his relational problems. Exacerbating his awkward bashfulness.

Though lacking excitement, the college year experience proved to Theo he could hold his own, mentally, among the students, even the most exalted ones. He had found himself somewhat—which was the reason Miss. Fielding had given in persuading Theo to go to the University.

"Education," Dreiser once explained, but a "selective presentation of certain stored or canned phases"—at best elucidative, at worse, a polishing process offered to experience—always basic. Experience, "the only teacher." Yo, John Dewey!

On returning to Chicago Theo become involved with a real estate agent. The agent however, too incompetent to last long in the field, and did not. Though Theo made out on the deal, for on one slow business day a young lady entered the office and Theo successfully bedded her in a back room. The success his realization he not impotent (as he feared). Not premature—but "normal!" The success set him to day-dreaming of harems he might conquer—bagnio's, bevies, of girls!

The mother died, aged fifty-eight. A great loss in that she the glue held the children in the nest.

Theo moved on to laundry wagon driver, a job Clyde Griffths also held, also in Chicago.

Despite the long work hours Theo continued to study in free moments. Also, his old Indiana University student-friend Sutcliff—he of the Hindoo-calm, was in Chicago and in contact—as well as Miss Fielding, stull urging her star pupil in the use of his mind. Reading the work of Robert Louis Stevenson and Leo Tolstoy inspiring Theo too, as did many of the lecturers he heard—giving mostly free talks here and there in the city.

Theo also had a girlfriend at this time—from the laundry: a Scotch Presbyterian, Nellie MacPherson, dreaming of children and marriage with hypercritical parvenu Theo ("a nibbling ass" he called himself) stringing the girl along in her dreams.

From the laundry Theo moved on to the pay-on-installment plan racket, as collector of time payments from those who joined the plan. The victims.

The loss of this job come about after Theo purloined $25 in payments to buy himself an overcoat, was caught, and fired. He never tried that trick again!

DAWN was one of Dreiser's best books. Written in sometimes poetic language, and mostly crystalline prose.

NEWSPAPER DAYS

First published, by Horace Liveright, in 1922, though under the title A BOOK OF MYSELF. Liveright cut 30,000 words from the original 900-page manuscript but the University of Pennsylvania Press republication, published in 1991, restored most of the cuts.

Not nearly as well written a work as DAWN, NEWSPAPER DAYS had its charm—particularly in the wealth of anecdotal material included. Fast-paced, genial, looser in style than its successor (the work vol. 2 of the autobiography but published a decade previous to vol. 1, DAWN), the book picked up the story where Dreiser left off in DAWN.

It was Rousseau's CONFESSIONS that really moved Dreiser to the autobiographical mode. The frank analysis of the Frenchman's character and motivations used by Dreiser as a sort of template for his own revelations.

The mother's dying had thrown the children and father—living in a flat on Halstead Street in Chicago—into confusion and rancor and recrimination. The father powerless to establish discipline or even order. Warring egos of the children precipitated a crisis: Theo, along with two younger siblings, Ed and Claire (Tillie), moved out into another apartment.

When the apartment failed, Theo and Ed boarded with a family while Claire moved into a rooming house room.

During this period, late 1880's-1893, Theo believing himself "impotent." Because of premature ejaculation he feeling he could not satisfy, physically, a woman—no penetration—thus, "impotent." (This feeling continuing, despite at least one non-impotent coupling.)

Dreiser's career as newspaper reporter begun in Chicago, continuing in Saint Louis, Pittsburgh, and New York City. Giving the lowdown, scoop, skinny. Surviving in the world of so-called "yellow journalism."

It was while working in Saint Louis Dreiser first felt stirrings of literary ambition. Shown a fellow newsman's novel, Dreiser begun thought he might write something too—not novel, but possibly a play. Talk and friendship with newspaper writers and artists created an encouraging milieu for him to write. He begun not with play but poetry—referring to his efforts as "jingling slush." The small circle of other writers and artists become Dreiser's Bohemia. His "Academy of Plato at Athens," he wrote.

A horrific train crash and explosion of oil tanks in which many were burnt, maimed, and killed, made Dreiser's reputation as skilled reporter after, on his own initiative, he made his way to the site and wrote a stirring objective account of the horror. A pay raise ensued, plus $20 bonus—when a sawbuck was a sawbuck, mister!

Because of excellent work Theo was able to have himself named the newspaper's Drama Critic. One night when three new shows were to arrive in town—and Theo unable to attend, due to other reportorial duties—he ghost-wrote 3-reviews—a common enough practice—only none of the shows were performed, the companies having been stranded along the road! In embarrassment, he resigned from the newspaper, later catching on with a different paper, for less money, and with bad timing, as the depression 1893 in progress.

Dreiser at his anecdotal best in this chatty-volume. Characters and incidents galore, including his long drawn-out courtship of his wife.

A visit to Saint Louis by his brother Paul put the bug for NYC into Theo's head. Paul Dresser, Falstaffian song & dance man, writer of the sentimental ballad par excellence, sang praises of the bright lights and freedom of opportunity for creative types in the multi-armed robotic city of the world. A tune Theo heeded, decamping Saint Louis for an around the country tour before arriving, a year or so later, after stops in Toledo, Cleveland, Buffalo, and Pittsburgh, in the Big Apple.

Liveright re-published NEWSPAPER DAYS in 1930 as companion volume to DAWN.

DUSK

Dreiser again drew from his money cow, Hollywood, making $25,000 in allowing a film version of JENNIE GERHARDT to be made. Surprisingly, Dreiser approved of the film. Unfortunately for him however, Liveright had gone under and JENNIE was unavailable in stores, copies of the novel and other of Dreiser's novels languishing in Liveright's stockroom.

Like other CP sympathizers, Dreiser had a hard time rationalizing the repulsive murderous acts of comrade Stalin. Believing however, that the Soviet experiment must succeed, Dreiser tempered his criticism, and refused any whole-hearted support of defamed exiled and murdered Trotskyists. Dreiser was said to have a guarded admiration for Hitler (pg. 407, Swanberg), mostly because the Fuehrer likewise hated the English, and also because he was out to settle the Jewish question. Dreiser had an animus against Jews, mostly because of treatment he received by the ones he had had to deal with in Hollywood—also in the publishing business. An anti-Semitic bias though with many good personal relationships with Jewish people.

During those years—1930-40, and afterwards, Dreiser was a "confused angry ex-artist," W. A. Swanberg wrote, "speaking out a psychopathic pot pourri of prejudice and zeal." (An "emotional visionary" type.)

A new publisher, Simon & Schuster, was contracted with. The company published a collected edition of Dreiser's often slight little tower-shaped poems. The book titled MOODS (why not FOOTPRINTS IN THE SAND?). A contractual relationship that quickly soured in the face of Dreiser's increasing demands—such as demand for publication of a uniform edition of all his books.

Dreiser went to Spain in '38 to speak at a conference of American Writers. Also published, at this time, a book titled THE LIVING THOUGHTS OF THOREAU, finding common ground with the sage of Walden Pond, with shared love of nature and perceived theological similarities of thought.

Dreiser sold, through an agent, film rights to SISTER CARRIE and "My Brother Paul" (of TWELVE MEN), raking in nearly $100,000 (pg. 383, Loving).

Teaming again with Helen, the couple first lived in Glendale, CA, then in West Hollywood, and finally—in Dreiser's 2nd and last house, in Hollywood.

As war threatened—the Big One, WW II—Dreiser became part of the "America First" movement, a Donald Trump-like amalgamation spearheaded by Charles "Lindy" Lindbergh. In a book—the forgettable AMERICA IS WORTH SAVING, an extended mostly ghost-written pamphlet (like Celine's pre-war pamphlets of notoriety), Dreiser tore England a new you-know-what. An Anglophobic account claiming England no different than Germany. A view causing the FBI to secretly recommend that Dreiser be put in "custodial detention in event of a national emergency" (pg. 386, Loving).

After the Nazi-German invasion of the Soviet Union, 1941, Theo got off his pro-Hitler/Germany spiel to roundly condemn the Fuehrer for having ambitions to empire (though not lessening his Anglophobia). After the "dastardly" attack of the Japanese Empire on Pearl Harbor, Dreiser urged all Americans to pull together, referring to the country as "democratic in spirit"—if not financially (pg. 430, Lingeman, vol. 2).

Dreiser broke from Simon & Schuster for Putnam & Sons, who called for the long-awaited novel THE BULWARK, which existed in 4-separate versions, all written before 1920 (pg. 431, Lingeman).

Meanwhile, Dreiser's wife, Sara White, 'Jug,'—who had never agreed to a divorce—and had been collecting $200 monthly in alimony, died. Aged seventy-three (1942).

Dreiser's financial worries slowed work on THE BULWARK. He willing to write articles for as little as $100 in this period until a check for $35,000 arrived from the Soviet Union—royalties accrued on his books published in Russia (pg. 443, Lingeman, vol, 2).

By March, 1943, Dreiser had completed 34-chapters of his novel (pg. 390, Loving) THE BULWARK. He also broke from his most recently engaged publisher, Putnam, over failure of the firm to contract for a uniform edition of his works (the wartime paper shortage made such effort undoable).

THE BULWARK derived from a story Anna Tatum, one time Dreiser lover and associate, had told him, concerning her Quaker father. Dreiser's interest in returning to the long-embryonic work not so much for art—which he seemed done with—but to espouse his new philosophical-theological ideas, including those he had considered in his Thoreau study—Thoreauvian notions similar to his, Dreiser's, religio-theological evolution. The "Creative Force" rather than or in place of "God" providing experience of life to all existence. Quakerism paralleling some of Dreiser's idea of such a force—in the Quaker's belief in an "inner light" (as Buddhism does in claim of Buddha-nature inherent and available to all).

Marguerite Tjader Harris, long-time Dreiser collaborator, called-upon to come west and assist in production of the novel. Helen gave the OK for Marguerite to come. Dreiser and Marguerite cut through the 4-extant typescripts and stitched together a manuscript.

Vera Dreiser, Theo's brother Ed's daughter, a psychiatrist, diagnosed her Uncle, at this time, as having "Oedipal longings," and wrote "a supporting mother and surrogate (like Helen) was the image sought by him (Dreiser) in a love relationship." Vera later wrote a book, MY UNCLE THEODORE, published in 1976.

THE BULWARK

Solon Barnes the Quaker Boy and Benecia Wallin, Quaker Girl, of the Religious Society of Friends.

Solon, son of Rufus and Hannah Barnes. Benecia, daughter and only child of Justus and Cornelia Wallin. The Barnes's come down into New Jersey from Maine. The Wallin's well-established, and wealthy—far more so than the Barnes's—in the Jersey-Philadelphia area.

Rufus and Solon entered the employ of Justus Wallins.

The love of Solon for Berenica, and vice-versa, grown in secrecy. Meanwhile, the Barnes-Wallin business making significant strides forward.

After a local banker tried to hire Rufus and Solon away from Wallin, Justus convinced Solon to come to Philadelphia, for more money, and to learn the banking business.

Solon eagerly seizing the opportunity—for the move gave him further proximity to Berenica.

A marriage between the two shortly proceeding. The couple living in a house on a farm of 25-acres, presented by the bride's parents.

Life, idyllic, commencing for the happily married couple. Solon as assistant bank manager, Berenica at home holding down the fort. Two incidents only to remark: death of Solon's mother, Hannah, and children born: Isobel, Orville, Dorothea Barnes.

A happy home life ensuing. Without art or music or movies or books of any kind except the Bible and various Quaker texts, such as "The Quaker Book of Discipline."

An unhappy incident marred the happy scene: endeavoring to help the son of a friend, Solon sponsored the boy into a lowly position with the bank. The boy committing a thievery bothering Solon to no end. Clyde Griffths-like, the boy stealing because overly restricted by Quaker parents, and eager to appease a desire for a different life. Samuel Griffths-like, Solon did nothing to ameliorate the severity of the boy's punishment—sentenced to 4-years in the penitentiary.

Rufus Barnes died. Solon inherited home and money (his sister had married and moved elsewhere).

One dead, another born: a daughter, Etta. Then a 5th child, a son, Stewart Barnes.

The oldest Barnes's child Isobel not as attractive a Barnes as the others. She bemoaning her condition as exception to the rule of handsome Barnes's. Her condition plus the crime of the wayward boy employee brought Solon to question why an all-merciful God allowed bad and unfortunate things to happen.

The children begun presenting innumerable problems for the parents. How were they, the parents, to keep the children on the farm after they, the children, had seen Philadelphia? Their clamor for worldly pleasures disturbed Solon, trying to shield the children from the sinful world at large. Benecia less troubled, but troubled nonetheless because of Solon's disquietude. Benecia kindly, quiet, self-effacing homebody; an extension of her husband and challenge to verisimilitude for a modern age-reader.

The children aided and abetted in their struggles to assimilate with the world of non-Friends through example and encouragement of Aunt Hester, self-motivated worldly spinster.

Solon and Benecia controlled their children's actions but not their thoughts. And their thoughts often strayed far from those held by George Fox and John Wollman and other Quaker exemplars.

Like Dreiser and his siblings rejecting their father's religiosity so too the Barnes's children. Etta. 4th child, went to live, with a companion, in Greenwich Village, becoming a model, and more, to a well-known village painter-artist. The youngest child, Stewart, rebellious by nature, and like the young Dreiser of DAWN hungry for physical sex gratification, was eager to play, finding companionship in characters of like-mind—mischievous fellows—among the students of his school. One of those characters, who had access to an automobile, taking Stewart and other boys and girls on a joy-ride about the area—Sparcer-like with Clyde and his Green-Davison pals.

One of the fun-seeking boys, in pursuit of his pleasure, gave one of the girls a Mickey-Finn that not only knocked her out but killed her. After leaving the body along the highway the panic-stricken boys returned to school and were picked-up there by police. Put into lock-up, Stewart Barnes used his pocket-knife to commit suicide in his cell.

Meanwhile, in Greenwich Village, Etta's affair with the painter ending, she returned like the prodigal child to her family.

Benecia had a stroke and died. Solon quit the bank due to practices by the bank he viewed as unethical. Soon afterward, he was diagnosed with cancer and was cared for by Isobel and Etta. Then he too died—though not before bringing Etta into the light, or The Light; the inner and guiding light of Quaker belief.

After Solon's funeral, Etta was discovered crying by cold and practical businessman and nominal Quaker, her brother Orville. He wanted to know why—as she—with her wayward lifestyle, the cause of so much family misery—Etta replying that she was "crying for LIFE!" A coda for the novel, and the empathetic reach of Dreiser's fiction.

SUI GENERIS

THE BULWARK unlike any other novel Dreiser wrote. A more compacted style—less rotund and labyrinthine sentences and without the authorial voice that spoke through Dreiser's other fictional productions. The work notable as well for the absence of such Dreiserism's as "whilom." "logy," "trig," "vagrom," "quondam," and "qui vive."

F.O Matthiessen wrote that the novel "is far more symbolical than naturalistic"—and for the better, I think.

ALL THAT REMAINED INSCRUTABLE

THE BULWARK (1946) sold well, netting Helen some $15,000 in royalties during initial months post-publication (pg. 527, Swanberg), and $40,000 total (pg. 481, Lingeman, vol.2)

Dreiser had married Helen in 1944. Helen the dutiful; the much-maligned; much put-down survivor of 25-years on and off with Dreiser, had arrived, outlasting the other women; at the summit, apotheosis of relationship: marriage. Now age fifty-one (Dreiser 74), plump, and "a little faded" (pg. 512, Swanberg) she attempted to help her husband complete THE STOIC, a novel long in gestation and said to be three-quarters completed at the time (pg. 472, Lingeman, vol. 2). Mrs. Harris also returned to the LA area to help—despite Helen's refusing to tolerate her presence.

James T. Farrell, novelist and heir to Dreiser's naturalism, was sent the manuscript and with a Doubleday editor made suggestions, later incorporated into the work.

In his last days Dreiser requested membership in the Communist Party (a request previously rejected) and was accepted. The request seemingly some sort of statement and affirmation of the Communist's stated utopian vision of human brother and sisterhood. A vision that badly floundered in the nearsightedness of Stalin and others. The Dreiser request, according to W. A. Swanberg, had also a religious basis reaffirming Dreiser's belief, however muddled by reality (his "not knowing the deity for what it was" (pg. 522, Swanberg)"—"the great Russian White Christ.") The request also an act of faith, Richard Lehan contended—faith in the possibility of utopia on earth.

Dreiser died of a heart attack 12-28-1945, leaving an estate valued over $100,000 (pg. 527, Swanberg). He was buried in Forest Lawn

Memorial Park, Los Angeles, CA. Helen died in 1951, leaving an estate of $184,000 (pg. 528, Swanberg).

In his will Dreiser had stipulated that on her death Helen bequeathed a certain percentage of the estate's income to a Negro orphanage of her selection (pg. 427, Swanberg).

THE STOIC (1947), Dreiser's last hurrah, was judged a "tired performance" by many critics (pg. 481, Lingeman, vol. 2). Judged so, I venture, because last chapters never received attention needed due to Dreiser's demise. The abrupt conclusion also a casualty of the demise.

THE STOIC

Berenice Fleming, whom Cowperwood—now nearing age sixty—had been dogging since the girl 12-years old, bestowed a ring upon her finger (not marriage—more concubinage).

Coming off his big defeat in Chicago—failing in a bid to have his franchise lease extended fifty years, Cowperwood decided to divest his Chicago holdings and went off to Europe seeking further accomplishments. First stop, and focus, London, and the feasibility of organizing the city's underground tube system.

Wary of the publicity sure to follow any adventure of his, and of reaction of Aileen, his wife—in name only; she living in Cowperwood's New York mansion—were she to surmise his current infatuation (Berenice, now of age) and so cause trouble—as in past episodes (like beating hell out of one of Frank's love-of-the-month girl's in Chicago).

Aileen the warrior-woman needed placating if Frank to carry-on in peace his nefarious liaisons, not only with Berenice but others of his harem, including some who lived in homes provided by Frank—who distributed houses and jewels like other men gave flowers.

Although much reduced, by alcohol and excess flesh, Aileen must be considered by Frank in avoidance of any unseemly actions intruding into his private sphere—thus the placating of her, the trophy wife in a sham marriage.

To this placating end Cowperwood engaged the service of one Bruce Tollifer, handsome but dissipated déclassé social dandy—formerly in good standing as one of the Tollifers of Virginia and South Carolina. Bruce engaged to provide social chaperonage to Aileen, keeping her, it was hoped, occupied and abstracted and out Cowperwood's thinning hair.

On board ship, Cowperwood, Aileen, Tollifer, and consort. A masquerade of smiles and polite remarks ensuing. A social farce arranged by arch-dissembler Cowperwood; of which, Aileen, a trifle vacant in upper stories (the reason Cowperwood had thrown her over) unaware of. (Berenice and her mother reaching London ahead of Frank & company.)

With the charade ongoing, business went on as usual: Frank set on taking over the tube business of London, beginning with negotiations galore with various and sundry Lyme's, some of whom averse to dealing with a foreigner showing interest in their isolated works. Even a foreigner as loaded with cash as Frank.

Taking delight in Berenice, admiring her beauty and mentality and spirit (a sensual spirited girl), Frank was both father and lover to the girl. (Did Dreiser have incestuous relations with his sisters? How honest his childhood accounting in DAWN?)

A lot of talk in THE STOIC. Far more than in the usual Dreiser production. Some of it worth hearing, some not so worthy.

Financial machinations between Cowperwood and English cabals of business me-Lords as fascinating and sometimes complex as machinations described in THE FINANCIER and THE TITAN.

With Aileen off to Paris with her new pre-planned and planted paramour or consort Tollifer, Frank and Bevy, and Bevy's Ma, were touring English cathedral towns.

The great farce continuing: Frank requesting Aileen accompany him back to NYC so he could beg or borrow money enough to buy the London underground. Continuing also the scam of Tollifer's pretense of affection for Aileen.

How the Mephistophelian charade would implode—once discovered!

Back in America, Cowperwood soon gathering enough funds for his London project—also gathering, in his arms, a new love interest, 19-year old Lorna, a dancer; attractive, sensual—and a relative! A grandniece—from the poorer Cowperwood branch. Frank, being Frank, wasted no time in reuniting with the family.

His "varietism" a flaming fever he was unable to treat. Berenice though still number one in his affection he told himself. So why this new interest, Frank thought—in a rare instancing of a bit, a fit, of self-analysis. Was he to blame? He wondered. But not for long, deciding the fever more powerful than he; he a victim of it (though not using the term "victim"). A rationalization, of course, from arch-rationalizing Cowperwood. A law onto himself—a god even, though a minor one (terrestrial); or is he demon? His abusing the feeling of others, demoniacal. Others not really human, seemingly; but material he could shape as he would…Process of a craven narcissism collapsing into an "I," hollowed at the core, and needing an "am"; as in "I am," to continue standing upright.

Ultimately, a sad condition—if not so lethal, emotionally, to those entering the world of Frank.

The new acquisition, Lorna, the dancer—of some repute—celebrated on New York stages—not as significant, thought Frank, as Berenice.

As with previous of Frank's conquests, he had Aileen invite the new girl to the home. Aileen coldly measuring her competition (not knowing, though suspecting, Berenice Fleming somewhere in the background).

Frank had his boy Tollifer return to New York from the continent—to placate Aileen. Aileen, meanwhile, coming upon a newspaper article connecting Frank and Lorna the dancer, mailed the article to Berenice—living at Pryor's Cove off the English coast. The cove property heirloom of the English Stanes; his Lord Stane, the latter, or latest, Landlord, boarding Berenice and mother, and making himself known to the young lady, in land-lordly fashion. His Lordship however, soon presenting a dilemma for Berenice: English nobility or noble, or notable, American savagery? Stane or Frank?

"Lady Stane" had a nice ring to it when spoken inside Berenice's pretty head. She and Stane's son would be Earl of Stane! But how she to explain to Stane the true nature of her "guardianship" with Cowperwood? Or her mother's nefarious past (Madam Hattie)?

Fearing Berenice's reaction to his published relations with Lorna, the grandniece, Cowperwood, with Aileen in tow, rushed back to England and Bevy.

Meanwhile—the plot thickening—Lord Stane falling half-in-love with Berenice, who, contemplating her guardian-lover and new admirer, deciding on the guardian—as the more forceful personage, with his "blazing force" and "nimbus" of power.

With returned Frank and Pryor Cove-Bevy trying to come to agreement over some type of future (he confessing all) Aileen come to knowledge of Tollifer's employer and the perpetrated scam. Volcanic Aileen: maybe not the brightest bulb among women but emotionally a force few others could match. She threatened to expose Frank's shenanigans publicly.

Cowperwood again crossing the ocean—for the 4th? 5th? 6th time? A five day voyage. In order to speak with Aileen in New York—bringing a lot of flattery and blarney and sweetening his deal by promising to place her in charge of the renovation of his art gallery—attached to the family mansion.

The diagnosis of Frank's "Bright's Disease"—old fashioned term for kidney disease, acute or chronic nephritis—and the prognosis of a year to live, changing everything—including the drama developed in previous pages. The only drama left becoming number of Frank's kidney attacks and time of his incipient death.

Frank's New York doctor was rowed over to England. Doctor James. Who knew? Providing yeoman service, unstinting devotion (and refusing his fee!). Who knew Frank had so good a friend? Or even had a friend?

Once again, back across the ocean for Frank, in the good ship Lolly-Pop. Frank arriving in a near-death condition.

Aileen, bedside, was told by Frank of his recently constructed tomb, built for he and Aileen to lie in in perpetuity—built to last 1000-years!

Aileen not so impressed, then angry—fit to be tied—after happening to spot Berenice in the hospital hallway, by the elevator doors.

The dirty! Dirty! She refusing further visits to the blackguard's bed; refusing to accept the casket of the deceased into the mansion.

Post-demise, Cowperwood's millions disappearing like May snow in New England.

The materialization of Doctor Saint-James an oddity—deus ex machina—equally odd Berenice's trip to India and her meeting a Hindoo guru whose talk read like gibberish.

CONCLUSION

Dreiser reached apotheosis of his literary endeavor with his 1925 publication AN AMERICAN TRAGEDY. In the following twenty years, until completion of THE BULWARD in 1945, nothing he wrote remotely equaled the power of the TRAGEDY. His opus plus SISTER CARRIE become classic—so too JENNIE GERHARDT to a less heralded extent. Some of Dreiser's short stories, such as "Nigger Jeff," "St. Columba and the River," and "The Lost Phoebe," could stand on their own feet in any American or world anthology. Due to its narrative thrust and other attributes (powerful romance) THE FINANCIER was the best of Dreiser's TRILOGY OF DESIRE. The first three-quarters of the autobiographical DAWN made for compelling reading, as did all of the essays in TWELVE MEN. THE BULWARK was a minor classic, truncated but yanking at heart strings as adamantly if not as long as any Dreiser novel. NEWSPAPER DAYS, 2nd volume of his autobiography is a baggy and verbose twin of the heavily, and unfortunately edited, A TRAVELER AT FORTY.

"The last great American writer of Melvillean dimensions," Jerome Loving wrote of Dreiser. Dimensionality and similarity in each writer's search to uncover and understand the phenomenon of existence. A spiritual quest though neither man having any sectarian belief (Melville nominally Unitarian). What and whom the 'oversoul' of Emersonian transcendentalism? To Dreiser, the grand protagonist LIFE itself suggesting a something else: God or gods perhaps, behind the display of natural phenomenon. Suggesting that God or gods, or "Creative Force," used humankind for his, her, its own purpose; a purpose hidden from humankind's limited understanding; also theorizing possibilities of additional God or gods in the background making use of, let us say, "primary" God or gods, for a like inscrutable purpose.

In last years Dreiser looking through a microscope for clues to the phenomenality of being—to unravel mysteries of life. Switching gears mid-career, he becoming an explorer of consciousness who preferred the company of scientists to that of literary brethren (to the detriment of his art, I must add).

In DAWN Dreiser theorized that humankind an invention—a schemed-out machine, useful to a larger something. A theory marking his turn from an early mechanistic belief in universal proceedings to consideration of an oversoul, or creative intelligence, behind or causative to universal phenomenon.

But what "soul"? What cause? What intelligence? Ahab tried to tear the veil that covered the quondam source; tried to expose the phenomenon of so-called "reality," but being only a man, and mortal, failed—dying in the process. What the symbolism of the great whale's whiteness but a concealing veil thrown over appearances? Melville's scientifically scrupulous dismantling of his leviathan part by part, yielding naught as to mysteries of origins and unquantifiable organic processes, but he, as Dreiser, wandering over the same dry speculative desert (as Hawthorne noted) each too honest to be or do otherwise.

Dreiser had his own mystic creed; refusing to conform to any formal doctrine—his views in later years influenced by Quakerism, Hinduism, and Christian Science (which his wife Jug, and Eugene Witla came under spell of). In NEWSPAPER DAYS, and in a sour mood, he wrote "religion! What a mockery! Why pray? Of whom to ask? The one who loaded the dice at the start?" Elsewhere in that same book—and in a better mood—he wrote "there is a sower somewhere. Is it planet, gas, element, fire? It gardens and sows—what is its plan, and why?"

Like many ex-parochial students, Dreiser had a profound dislike of Catholicism and her rituals. A dislike engendered, in Dreiser's case, by scorn of the ineffectual father, John Paul Dreiser. In DAWN Dreiser wrote of Catholics with ossified brains who rejected natural emotion as sinful; who spent inordinate amounts of time on their knees praying to an immense and inscrutable something which cared not for their adoration or supplication.

He denied sectarian pretense to divine authority and wrote about how little there was to the Christ legend aside from artistic spectacle. Ritual and churchly dogma infuriated him—particularly angered by the priest who at first denied Dreiser's mother burial in the sacred grove because she being a lapsed Catholic.

Dreiser despised religion in the form of Catholicism as much as he come to despise oligarchy—though early in his career celebrated the power of the oligarch in the character of Frank Cowperwood, apotheosis of laissez faire capitalism run amuck.

Will Dreiser's work survive the muddle of brave new world exigencies? I hope so. The slow relentless and inexorable pace of his stories, with their accumulation of details, are or seem anathema to the cyborg-screed of flash fiction sound bites in the blogosphere, but the stories he told—all having to do with vagaries of the human heart—though perhaps out of vogue, will never not be relevant to the human oh so human condition.

SELECTED BILIOGRAPHY

DREISER, W. A. Swanberg, Charles Scribner & Sons, New York, N.Y., 1965.

THEODORE DREISER, At the Gates of the City, 1871-1907, Vol. 1, Richard Lingeman, G. P. Putnam's Sons, New York, N. Y., 1986.

THEODORE DREISER, An American Journey, 1908-1945, Vol 2, Richard Lingeman, G. P. Putnam's Sons, New York, N. Y., 1990.

THE LAST TITAN, A Life of Theodore Dreiser, Jerome Loving, University of California Press, Irvine, CA, 2005.

THEODORE DREISER: Our Bitter Patriot, Charles Shapiro, Southern Illinois University Press, Carbondale, Ill., 1962.

THEODORE DREISER, His World and His Novels, Richard Lehan, Southern Illinois University Press, Carbondale, Ill., 1969.

THEODORE DREISER, F.O. Matthiesson, American Men of Letters Series, William Sloane Asso. Inc., 1951.

LITERARY MASTERS, Theodore Dreiser, Vol. 7, Gale Study Guides to Great Literature, Donald Pizer, Henry Holt & Company, New York, N. Y., 2000.

AMERICAN NERVOUSNESS, 1903, An Anecdotal History, Tom Lutz, Cormell University Press, Ithaca, New York, 1991.

CRITICAL WORKS

THEODORE DREISER'S AN AMERICAN TRAGEDY, Interpretations, Editor Harold Bloom, Chelsea House Publisher, New York, N Y., 1988.

DREISER'S JENNIE GERHARDT, New Essays on the Restored Text, Editor James L. W. West III, University of Pennsylvania Press, Philadelphia, 1995.

THEODORE DREISER, Editor James T. Farrell, Dell Paperbacks, New York, N. Y., 1962.

ADDITIONAL READING

THE SKEPTIC, A Life of H. L. Mencken, Terry Teachout, Perennial, Imprint of Harper Collins Pub., New York, N. Y., 2002.

FRANK NORRIS, A Life, Joseph R. McElrath Jr. and Jesse S Crisler, University of Illinois Press, Urbana, Ill., 2006.

BURNING BOY, The Life and Work of Stephen Crane, Paul Auster, Henry Holt & Company, New York, N. Y., 2021.

DREISER'S WORKS

AN AMERICAN TRAGEDY, Theodore Dreiser, Horace Liveright, 1925, Signet Classics, Penguin Group, New York, N. Y., 1964.

A HOOSIER HOLIDAY, Theodore Dreiser, Indiana University Press, Bloomington and Indianapolis, Indiana, 1997.

THE GENIUS, Theodore Dreiser, Robinia Classics, United States, 1915.

A TRAVELER AT FORTY, Theodore Dreiser, University of Illinois Press, Urbana and Chicago, Ill., Editor Renate von Bardelebon, 2004.

JENNIE GERHARDT, Theodore Dreiser, Oxford University Press, 1991. Originally published 1911, Harper Brothers.

SISTER CARRIE, Theodore Dreiser, Editor Blaude Simpson, Houlton Mifflin Company, New York, N. Y., 1959.

TWELVE MEN, Theodore Dreiser, Fawcett Publisher, 1962. Originally published Boni & Liveright, New York, N. Y., 1919.

DAWN, Theodore Dreiser, Horace Liveright Inc., New York, N. Y., 1931.

NEWSPAPER DAYS, Theodore Dreiser, Editor T. D. Nostwich, University of Pennsylvania Press, Philadelphia, 1991.

THEODORE DREISER, American Diaries 1902-1926, Editor Thomas P. Riggio, University of Pennsylvania Press, Philadelphia, 1983.

THEODORE DREISER, Best Short Stories, Elephant Paperbacks, 1999. Originally published 1947.

Wayne F. Burke writes both poetry and prose. He is the author of nineteen published books, including twelve poetry collections, one short story collection, a novella, and five works of non-fiction—most recently "the VAN GOGH file: POTATOE EATERS, PREACHERS, and PAINTERS" (Cyberwit.net. Press, 2024). He lives in Vermont (USA).

www.ingramcontent.com/pod-product-compliance
Ingram Content Group UK Ltd.
Pitfield, Milton Keynes, MK11 3LW, UK
UKHW041314190726
13845UKWH00025B/251

9 789363 542716